# Fast Facts on Defending Your Faith

## John Ankerberg
## &John Weldon

HARVEST HOUSE™PUBLISHERS

EUGENE, OREGON

Cover by Terry Dugan Design, Minneapolis, Minnesota

## FAST FACTS ON DEFENDING YOUR FAITH

A revised edition of *Ready with an Answer* and *Knowing the Truth About Salvation*
Copyright © 2002 by John Ankerberg and John Weldon
Published by Harvest House Publishers
Eugene, Oregon 97402

Library of Congress Cataloging-in-Publication Data
Ankerberg, John, 1945–
    Fast facts on defending your faith / John Ankerberg and John Weldon.
        p.  cm.
Includes bibliographical references.
        ISBN 0-7369-1056-5 (pbk.)
    1. Apologetics. I. Weldon, John. II. Title.
    BT1103 .A55 2002

                                                                2002003154

Printed in the United States of America.

02   03   04   05   06   07   08   09   10   / BC-CF /   10   9   8   7   6   5   4   3   2   1

To Richard G. Boyer

**Author's note:** This book is part of a series of short "Fast Facts" books designed to help the reader understand the basic facts that support the claims and the truth of Christianity. Some books in the series will deal with the evidence directly and some with evaluating the claims of other faiths or movements. Some readers may want to explore some of the questions posed in more detail.

For deeper study, the reader is encouraged to seek out many of the fine books listed in the extensive notes section at the end of this book, especially the following:

Origins.org

LeadershipU.com

Probe.org

Tektonics.org

BiblicalDefense.org

Discovery.org

Phillip E. Johnson, *Reason in the Balance: The Case Against NATURALISM in Science, Law & Education* (Downer's Grove, IL: InterVarsity, 1995).

John Warwick Montgomery (ed.), *Evidence for Faith: Deciding the God Question* (Dallas: Probe/Word, 1991).

Cal Beisner, *Answers: For Atheists, Agnostics and Other Thoughtful Skeptics* (Wheaton, IL: Crossway, 1993).

Henry Margenau and Roy Abraham Varghese, eds., *Cosmos, Bios, Theos: Scientists Reflect on Science, God and the Origin of the Universe, Life and Homo Sapiens* (LaSalle, IL: Open Court, 1992).

Norman L. Geisler, *Baker Encyclopedia of Christian Apologetics* (Grand Rapids, MI: Baker Books, 1999).

Ravi Zacharias, *Can Man Live Without God?* (Dallas: Word, 1994).

Norman L. Geisler, (ed.), *Inerrancy* (Grand Rapids, MI: Zondervan, 1980).

Paul Johnson, "The Necessity of Christianity" (Leaderu.com/truth/1truth08.html).

Ajith Fernando, *The Supremacy of Christ* (Wheaton, IL: Crossway, 1995).

Francis J. Beckwith and Michael E. Bauman eds. *Are You Politically Correct? Debating America's Cultural Standards* (Prometheus, 1993).

R.C. Sproul, *Not a Chance: The Myth of Chance in Modern Science and Cosmology* (Grand Rapids, MI: Baker Books, 1994).

W.R. Bird, *The Origin of Species Revisited*, 2 vol. (New York: Philosophical Library, 1993).

# Fast Facts on
# Defending
# Your Faith

## John Ankerberg
## &John Weldon

HARVEST HOUSE™ PUBLISHERS

EUGENE, OREGON

Cover by Terry Dugan Design, Minneapolis, Minnesota

**FAST FACTS ON DEFENDING YOUR FAITH**
A revised edition of *Ready with an Answer* and *Knowing the Truth About Salvation*
Copyright © 2002 by John Ankerberg and John Weldon
Published by Harvest House Publishers
Eugene, Oregon 97402

Library of Congress Cataloging-in-Publication Data
Ankerberg, John, 1945–
    Fast facts on defending your faith / John Ankerberg and John Weldon.
        p.  cm.
Includes bibliographical references.
    ISBN 0-7369-1056-5 (pbk.)
    1. Apologetics. I. Weldon, John. II. Title.
    BT1103 .A55 2002

                                                                    2002003154

**Printed in the United States of America.**

    02    03    04    05    06    07    08    09    10    / BC-CF /    10    9    8    7    6    5    4    3    2    1

# CONTENTS

The immortality of the soul is a matter which is of so great consequence to us and which touches us so profoundly that we must have lost all feeling to be indifferent as to knowing what it is.

—Blaise Pascal

I start with being on bended knee every morning—seriously.

—President George W. Bush

Between us and heaven or hell there is only life, which is the frailest thing in the world.

—Blaise Pascal

# THE SEARCH
# FOR TRUTH

This book is written for people interested in truth—for those who already believe in God, for those who don't, for the searching, and for the skeptical who may doubt that truth even exists, but still find themselves curious.

This book is actually about *finding* the truth. Few things are more important. Most people already suspect there is more to life than meets the eye, so if finding the truth is possible, such people already have an interest. Some may have been diverted by the many pleasures in life, by skeptical philosophies, or by the will to disbelieve, but in the end, no one can escape their own curiosity or the suspicion that death does not end it all. It seems the world is too large for us, and its pleasures too small; something transcending this world is likely to be in order. Noted skeptical philosopher Bertrand Russell, the author of *Why I Am Not a Christian and Other Essays*, once wrote in a letter, "The centre of me is always and eternally a terrible pain—a curious wild pain—a searching for something beyond what the world contains, something transfigured and infinite."[1] We can see indications of this searching for something greater than ourselves all around us, either positively or negatively, in cinema, literature, science, education, philosophy, art, literature, politics, and most other realms of human endeavor.

If truth exists—and it does—it seems the worst possible outcome would be to live one's life without it. Indeed, as was so powerfully demonstrated by the September 11, 2001 horror, life can be unpredictably short. As Plato declared, "Truth is the beginning of every good thing, both in Heaven and on earth; and he who would be blessed and happy should be from the first a partaker of the truth."

But this is not a book about convenient truth, which is another word for making truth one's personal interest or preference. It's about taking the truth that is there—absolute truth—even if it may, in places, be hard to accept.

Of all things in life, knowing the truth is one of the most satisfying. Knowing the truth means knowing that what you believe is absolutely unshakeable—not just true for you alone, but for everyone. Not just now, but *forever.*

That's the only kind of truth worth having.

# Atheism, Agnosticism, and Faith

---

### 1

## Is Atheism Credible?

*Our repugnance to death increases in proportion to our consciousness of having lived in vain.*

**William Hazlett**

Since the dawn of time, human beings have been incurably religious, constantly asking such questions as Who am I? Why am I here? Where did I come from? What happens when I die? These are unavoidably religious questions and underscore the fact that human history is the history of religion—mankind's attempt to find satisfying answers to these questions. That thousands of libraries are dedicated to this search underscores the fact that there is perhaps no more valued possession than the truth. I (Weldon) can still remember sitting on the South Mission Beach sea wall in San Diego, a relativist and skeptic, just musing about things. I would look out at the sunset sometimes and have a sober conversation with myself, wondering what life was all about. What was I doing here anyway? I could never get past why there was something rather than nothing. My intuitive sense that nothing should exist was appropriate. Having unexamined biases that rejected the religious realm as a source of possible answers, I had literally nowhere to go but to agnosticism, insecurity, and a few more beers.

There have been many attempts to prove God's existence by philosophers and scholars old and new. Readers who want to wrestle with this basic question at considerable length are urged to seek out these arguments for more in-depth study than this brief book allows. However, let's take a quick look at some of the conclusions reached by those who have pondered this weighty question.

Sir Isaac Newton, one of the greatest scientists of history, observed, "He must be blind who from the most wise and excellent contrivances of things cannot see the Infinite Wisdom and Goodness of their Almighty Creator, and he must be mad and senseless who refuses to acknowledge them."[2] C.B. Anfinsen, Ph.D. (biochemistry, Harvard), Nobel Prize winner in chemistry, put it more succinctly when he wrote, "I think only an idiot can be an atheist."[3]

If many of the greatest intellects of history have believed in God, then it seems a bit presumptuous for anyone to claim with absolute assurance there is no God.[4] It is up to those who would make such a claim to prove their assertion. Atheists and skeptics never have offered proof that God does not exist, and they never will. To do so they would need omniscience, an attribute of deity. The logical problems and disproofs of atheism are well documented, and cannot be discussed here.[5] In truth, it is atheism that is irrational and logically indefensible, not theism. As the French genius Pascal said of atheists, "What reason have they for saying that we cannot rise from the dead? What is more difficult, to be born or to rise again; that what has never been should be, or that what has been should be again?"[6] While the failure of atheism does not prove any particular view of God, it does say a great deal about skeptical views that characteristically reject theism and supernaturalism as "proven myths." And it does logically require an openness to the evidence that tells us God does exist.[7]

As former atheist and psychologist Dr. Paul Vitz of New York University shows in "The Psychology of Atheism," atheists usually aren't atheists because of rational concerns about God's existence or evidential problems with Christianity, but primarily for psychological reasons.

> ...it is now clear to me that my reasons for becoming and for remaining an atheist-skeptic from about age 18 to 38 were superficial, irrational, and largely without intellectual or moral integrity. Furthermore, I am convinced that my motives were, and still are, commonplace today among intellectuals, especially social scientists....[8]

The vast majority of men and women throughout history have believed in God. As anthropologist Wilhelm Schmidt has documented (in 12 volumes and thousands of pages)[9] virtually every ancient culture carries at least a vestige of monotheism. Belief in one personal God was actually the original religion and a universal belief—a belief, incidentally, quite similar to Christian monotheism.[10] Even with a subsequent digression into polytheism in certain quarters, cultures and religions that believe in many gods still frequently believe in one supreme God ("Brahman" in Hinduism, for example). Belief in one personal God is still the dominant belief of humanity—Christians and Muslims alone comprise over half the world's population.

It is probably also true that the majority of the greatest thinkers among humanity, including scientists, have believed in God.[11] In light of this, one could argue that atheism is not the persuasive intellectual force its advocates claim. As to credibility, it would seem to be little more than an unsightly blemish on the face of history. Indeed, given the tremendously harmful consequences of nontheism in the last century alone[12] (far worse than those of even false theism), atheism and similar views are more than blemishes, they are actual cancers. Anyone who has not believed in God has always substituted something else for Him, and by necessity always something inferior. The truth is that unbelief has a lot to answer for. Undeniably, we find that at least 150 million unnecessary deaths in the last century is only the beginning.[13] For example, speaking of Hitler, Marx, Stalin and others, Professor Paul Johnson remarks: "What is so notable about the twentieth century, and a principal cause—I think *the* principal cause—of its horrors, is that great physical power has been acquired by men who have no fear of God and who believe themselves restrained by no absolute code of conduct."[14]

Many people from all professions and walks of life who do not embrace any particular religion still believe in God. People believe in God because they find it difficult to do anything else—the evidence is seemingly everywhere. In the daytime, we cannot see the stars, but we know they exist—we see them at night. Someone who lives at the North Pole, where light shines 24 hours a day and it is never night, might not believe in stars because he has never seen them. Still, they would exist as massive, awesome realities. The fact that we cannot yet see something (God) does not mean it (He) does not exist or that the evidence for His existence is lacking. Whether in science, philosophy, literature, or the hearts of people both common and famous, belief in God is almost universal.

In one reported study, lie detector tests were allegedly administered to several thousand people. One question was, "Do you believe in God?" "In every case, when a person answered no, the lie detector said he was lying."[15] We mention this because a new science is, allegedly, almost perfectly accurate in detecting lying. If split-second facial response photography were used to test thousands of atheists, the results might prove interesting indeed.

Perhaps our biggest folly would be to ignore the God who is there, the God everyone knows is there, and to live our lives as if He were irrelevant. It is folly because it is a kind of intuitive and intellectual suicide.

We all live out our lives more or less consistently with what we think is true. And, depending on what we believe, this has major implications for each of our lives, either positive or negative. Further, we all die. To live our lives apart from the truth isn't healthy, but to die without the truth is a tragedy. As the "Life is hell and then you die" T-shirt suggests, in the end, with all its trials and tribulations, life would hardly seem worth the trouble, unless one really did discover the truth.

---

### 2

## ARE ATHEISTS AND SKEPTICS COVERT BELIEVERS?

As noted, everyone believes in God no matter what they say, and this can be illustrated in atheists and skeptics as well. Even when skeptics say that they aren't certain of God's existence or that they disbelieve in God, they still know He exists. Although many examples could be cited, we offer one prominent illustration, that of the late Nobelist, leading French existentialist, and most eminent atheist of the twentieth century, Jean-Paul Sartre. Sartre confessed the following in an interview just before his death, published in the February, 1984 issue of *Harper's* magazine: "Even if one does not believe in God, there are elements of the idea of God that remain in us."[16] Sartre goes on to state, even though he had been a convinced atheist from the age of eight or nine, that the nature of consciousness and his own intuitive awareness and experience in life virtually compelled him to accept the existence of God: "As for me, I don't see myself as so much dust that has appeared in the world but as a being that was expected, prefigured, called forth. In short, as a being that could, it seems, come only from a creator; and this idea of a creating hand that created me refers me back to God. Naturally this is not a clear, exact idea that I set in motion every time I think of myself. It contradicts many of my other ideas; but it is there, floating vaguely. And when I think of myself I often think rather in this way, for wont of being able to think otherwise."[17]

Sartre couldn't help thinking about God in spite of his atheism. He knew God existed, but somehow refused to acknowledge Him. This is reminiscent of Romans 1:20-21: "For since the creation of the world God's invisible qualities—his eternal power and divine nature—have been clearly seen, being understood from what has been made, so that men are without excuse. For although they knew God, they neither glorified him as God nor gave thanks to him, but their thinking became futile and their foolish hearts were darkened." The term "since the creation of the world" includes all men and women who have ever lived. It doesn't say God has placed a knowledge of Himself in everyone except atheists and skeptics.

One reason the Bible spends no time arguing for God's existence is it simply isn't necessary. God has placed an innate knowledge of Himself within all men and confirmed it through the creation. Thus, God is "The true light that gives light to every man" (John 1:9). Even as a leading atheist, one who turned many to atheism, someone like Sartre could never escape God because he had not only been created, he had been created "in God's image" (Genesis 1:26-27). God had placed the knowledge of Himself directly into the being of Sartre. So, even though Sartre further stated, "This life owes nothing to God," he actually knew intuitively that his atheism was little more than his personal choice to pay no attention to God.

As Scripture teaches, everyone is the offspring of God, if God is not far from us, if we have our being in Him, if everyone is made in His image, and if God has "enlightened," and "made Himself known" to every person who has ever lived, then God has hardly been "silent," as Sartre argued. Indeed, His invisible qualities of eternal power and divine nature are "clearly seen, being *understood*" through the creation. As astronaut John Glenn declared from space on November 1, 1998, "For me to look out this window and see the earth there and not believe in God is *impossible*."[18]

What this means is that a lot of skeptics know more than they are saying. The occult psychologist Carl Jung, whose damage inflicted on Christianity was not small, wrote in his autobiography, *Memories, Dreams, Reflections*, "I find that all my thoughts circle around God like the planets around the sun, and are as irresistibly attracted by Him. I would feel it to be the grossest sin if I were to oppose any resistance to this force."[19]

If all this is true, then everyone knows there is a God, and they also know certain things about Him. Since God Himself has been their teacher, there is hardly a possibility of failure. There are no atheists or skeptics, finally, in foxholes, crashing airplanes, operating rooms, or anywhere else. There are only those who deny what they already know because, for whatever reason, they find it desirable to do so.

3

---

## ARE AGNOSTICISM AND RELATIVISM CREDIBLE?

While atheism makes the absolute statement, "God does not exist," agnosticism maintains that if God does exist, we cannot know it—that nothing can be known about the existence of God.

While different types of agnosticism exist, they can be reduced to three basic forms:

- Agnostics who make the absolute statement that it is impossible to know if God exists

- Agnostics who do not care if God exists

- Agnostics who don't know if God exists, but would be open to the evidence

Agnostics who say it is absolutely impossible to know if God exists have the same problem as the atheist—they are appealing to an absolute position that cannot be defended because such knowledge would require omniscience, an attribute of deity.

Agnostics who do not care whether God exists are perhaps only depressed, as God is clearly the most important subject there is. Anyone not interested in such a relevant, crucial, and fascinating issue should perhaps go to bed for a few days and get some rest. Indeed, Pascal had little sympathy for such an approach to life:

> This carelessness in a matter which concerns themselves, their eternity, their all, moves me more to anger than pity;

it astonishes and shocks me…We do not require great education of the mind to understand that here [in this life] is no real and lasting satisfaction; that our pleasures are only vanity; that our evils are infinite; and, lastly, that death, which threatens us every moment, must infallibly place us within a few years under the dreadful necessity of being for ever either annihilated or unhappy.

And he further emphasized:

There is nothing more real than this, nothing more terrible. Be we as heroic as we like, that is the end which awaits the world….[as to] the doubter who does not seek…I have no words to describe so silly a creature. How can people hold these opinions? What joy can we find in the expectation of nothing but hopeless misery? What reason for boasting that we are in impenetrable darkness? And how can it happen that the following argument occurs to a reasonable man? "I know not who put me into the world, nor what the world is, nor what I myself am. I am in terrible ignorance of everything. I know not what my body is, nor my senses, nor my soul, not even that part of me which thinks what I say, which reflects on all and on itself, and knows itself no more than the rest. I see those frightful spaces of the universe which surround me, and I find myself tied to one corner of this vast expanse, without knowing why I am put in this place rather than in another, nor why the short time which is given me to live is assigned to me at this point rather than at another of the whole eternity which was before me or which shall come after me. I see nothing but infinites on all sides, which surround me as an atom and as a shadow which endures only for an instant and returns no more. All I know is that I must soon die, but what I know least is this very death which I cannot escape….And from all this I conclude that I ought to spend all the days of my life without caring to inquire into what must happen to me"…

Who would desire to have for a friend a man who talks in this fashion? Who would choose him out from others to tell him of his affairs?...It is an incomprehensible enchantment...There must be a strange confusion in the nature of man, that he should boast of being in that state in which it seems incredible that a single individual should be.[20]

One would hope that agnostics and others who don't care about God might learn the obligation of interest. As to the third type of agnostic, those open to the evidence, hopefully they will also wish to consider the material in this book.

In any event, whether here or somewhere else, even hardened atheists, agnostics and other skeptics will have to be careful. As one-time atheist and Oxford scholar C. S. Lewis recalled prior to his own conversion: "A young man who wishes to remain a sound atheist cannot be too careful of his reading. There are traps everywhere— 'Bibles laid open, millions of surprises,' as Herbert says, 'Fine nets and stratagems.' God is, if I may say it, very unscrupulous."[21]

But most people today argue that whatever one's religion, it is right and true for them. This idea comprises what is known as a relativistic approach to religion. Relativism is the belief that each individual determines truth and reality for himself. It is perhaps the single most dominant secular philosophy in the West and conceivably the most damaging. Indeed, a variety of critiques have documented its consequences in depth.[22] Unfortunately, what relativists seem not to have realized is that if their philosophy is true, then everything is irrelevant, and absurd besides— including their own philosophy. As William D. Watkins points out, if "all truth is relative" and everyone is right, then no one is ever wrong—no matter how ridiculous, perverse, or immoral their beliefs. Those who believe in a square earth, molesting children, or human sacrifice are just as right as everyone else. Further, if relativism is true, reality itself is contradictory and meaningless—the Holocaust is both a fact of history and a mythical invention of Zionists; men went to the moon, and they never did. In fact, because no one can be wrong about anything, relativists can hardly attempt to challenge or correct the absolutist—who is just as right as they are. (The absolutist can logically seek to challenge and correct the relativist because the absolutist believes people can be wrong about their beliefs.) In addition, if relativism were true, no one could ever learn anything, including relativists. Learning presumes getting new knowledge and adjusting false beliefs. But relativism assumes all beliefs are true and none are false. So how does one learn anything in such a scheme of things? The fact that relativists do learn things undermines the legitimacy of their own philosophy. Finally, if all truth is relative, this includes all moral truth, which means no one should complain about crime or be angry when their loved ones are robbed or murdered by those who have the moral right to do so. On the other hand, if we say "all truth is relative" in another sense—that no one is absolutely right about anything—then even relativists must be wrong about relativism.[23]

The problem with relativism is that it is too bad to be true. And no one can live it consistently anyway. Everyone sometimes acts as if absolutes are true because they really are. Since relativism is obviously false and destructive, one assumes it would be better to consistently accept the idea that absolutes exist in the spheres of morality and truth. It seems life would be a lot easier for everyone.

---

### 4

## IS THE UNIVERSAL IMPRESSION OF WONDER A SENSING OF THE MIRACULOUS, AND IF SO, WHY DO MANY SIDESTEP THE IMPLICATIONS?

Biologist Lewis Thomas, M.D., president of the prominent Memorial Sloan-Kettering Cancer Center, wrote the following praise about the miracle of the fertilized human egg: "The mere existence of that cell should be one of the greatest astonishments of the earth. People ought to be walking around all day, all through their waking hours, calling to each other in endless wonderment, talking of nothing except that cell. If anyone does succeed in explaining it, within my lifetime, I will charter a skywriting airplane, maybe a whole fleet of them, and send them aloft to write one great exclamation point after another, around the whole sky, until all my money runs out."[24]

Dr. Thomas is quite correct. The ovum is indeed an astonishing miracle. And if the DNA content of just a single human body were printed as chemical "letters," and placed in a book, it would fill the Grand Canyon with books 50 times! But what about merely a single atom? Solitary atoms—one hydrogen atom being so small that 10,000 could be placed one on top of the other in the thickness of this piece of paper—have enough inherent power to produce an atomic bomb! The truth is there are literally tens of thousands of "miracles" everywhere we look. Walt Whitman, considered by many the greatest of all American poets, was correct in his intuitive observation that "every hour of the light and dark is a miracle. Every cubic inch of space is a miracle."[25]

The testimony of every good thing in life and creation is a testimony to the existence of God, and to His love, majesty, and goodness. Noted critic, poet, and philosopher Ralph Waldo Emerson, the seminal intellectual, philosophical voice of nineteenth century America once noted, "All I have seen teaches me to trust the Creator for all I have not seen."[26]

This awareness of wonder suggesting something miraculous, even in ordinary things, underscores the intuitive knowledge of God. Were we to interview everyone in the world, and each one spoke candidly, personal statements to this effect could be repeated six billion times. Distinguished movie director Frank Capra of "It's a Wonderful Life" fame is arguably the best director ever with six Best Director nominations and three Oscars; only John Ford bettered him with four. He makes the following astute observation: "As I got into the creative business, then I realized that creativity and God were connected, directly connected. Whether you believe in God or not. You had to believe, if you believed in creativity, you had to believe in some creator. And if you believed in some creator, where do you end up? You must go to that prime creator, which has set our universe in motion. Things are too ordered in the universe to be the result of chaos. There is no way you can get away from the fact that there's got to be some sort of divine idea to the whole thing."[27]

People everywhere make statements about God that have varying degrees of truth in them. This certainly says something about what people instinctively know about God. But an interesting point is that even though people know God is there, and that God has been good to them, they often pay little attention to Him! They know God exists (Romans 1:20), they "believe" in God, they realize God has been good to them—and yet many people live their lives largely as if He *doesn't* exist. Wonder of wonders. Perhaps people do this because they are either fearful or because they are willful. The sense of responsibility to a higher power seems to exist universally. So, if people know they fall short, and fear the consequences, they may seek to hide. Perhaps they distract themselves or invent beliefs to ease their concerns. Or perhaps they don't want to submit, even to a good and loving God. (Again, wonder of wonders.) As the esteemed philosopher Mortimer Adler recalled, prior to his own conversion to Christianity, "I simply did not wish to exercise a will to believe."[28] Famous novelist and skeptic Aldous Huxley wrote frankly that, "Most ignorance is vincible ignorance. We don't know because we don't want to know. It is our will that decides how and upon which subjects we shall use our intelligence."[29]

But it's getting harder and harder to hide.

------

## 5

## Does Science Provide Evidence of God and Confirm Faith?

In the end, there are only two major options for explaining our existence: the natural or the supernatural.

First, there is the supernatural or religious explanation. Is it reasonable to believe that the universe was created by an infinite

God? Second, there is the natural or evolutionary explanation. Is it more reasonable to believe the universe arose by chance from nothing, as much modern science claims? Interestingly enough, even the natural explanation is a religious one, tantamount to requiring faith in the miraculous. Either way we are forced into the realm of the religious. Further, if a great deal of scientific evidence rules out a naturalistic explanation for origins, we have little choice. By default we are automatically required to enter the realm of religious truth.

Evolutionary theory is the dominant scientific faith at the moment. However, belief in evolution and atheism are not necessarily equivalent. In fact, it is probably true that most evolutionists believe in some concept of a supreme being who used the process of evolution to create man. However, not only is the worldview of the atheistic evolutionist increasingly under scientific assault; so is that of the theistic evolutionist, and both for the same reason—any real evidence for evolution is lacking, as we documented in *Darwin's Leap of Faith*

It turns out that faith in naturalistic evolution is tantamount to faith in the miraculous. If atheistic scientists already believe in the miraculous, then perhaps only the will to disbelieve in God can account for their skepticism because belief in miracles is clearly not the problem. To be sure, modern science is a wonderful thing. Unfortunately, it is still often dominated by a false philosophy of naturalism that warps its interpretation of legitimate scientific data and by a philosophy of chance that will ruin it completely unless there is a reformation.[30]

Thankfully, the signs of that reformation are now emerging in the loosely related disciplines of the broadly based design movement, the more restricted field of theistic science, and the specific biblical creationist ("young earth") movement, which collectively may represent 50,000–75,000 scientists globally, perhaps more.[31] It is a fair statement to say that no matter how hard they try, materialistic scientists, atheists, and other skeptics can no longer logically avoid faith in the miraculous. A slew of recent books and articles are proof that even they are now being forced by the evidence to consider God and religious ideas when rationally explaining the origin of the universe.[32] Molecular biologist and medical doctor Dr. Michael Denton refers to the idea that evolution could occur by purely random processes (chance)—and yet produce the complexity of living organisms about us—as "simply an affront to reason."[33] It seems that tens of thousands of other scientists are beginning to agree with him. An impartial examination of twentieth-century scientific evidence has caused scores of world authorities to conclude that appealing to chance is equivalent to faith in supernatural miracles.

We return again to what is said in Romans 1:20—that the creation itself provides evidence concerning God's existence, evidence that is clearly seen and understood. Thus, "The evidence for a finite, decaying, and finely tuned universe has led many to conclude that there must be a Mind behind it all. Remarkably, many of these men are professed atheists who have been forced by the weight of twentieth-century discoveries in astronomy and physics to concede the existence of an intelligent Designer behind the creation of the universe."[34]

For example, Paul Davies was once a leader for the atheistic, materialistic worldview. He now asserts of the universe, "[There] is for me powerful evidence that there is something going on behind it all...It seems as though somebody has fine-tuned nature's numbers to make the Universe...The impression of design is overwhelming." Further, the laws of physics themselves seem "to be the product of exceedingly ingenious design."[35]

Astronomer George Greenstein observed, "As we survey all the evidence, the thought instantly arises that some supernatural agency—or, rather Agency—must be involved."[36]

In 1992, physicist and Nobel Laureate Arno Penzias noted, "Astronomy leads us to a unique event, a universe which was created out of nothing, one with the very delicate balance needed to provide exactly the conditions required to permit life, and one which has an underlying (one might say 'supernatural') plan."[37]

The term miracle is thus no longer restricted to creationist belief. Years ago, Nobel Prize-winning biochemist Dr. Francis Crick commented, "An honest man, armed with all the knowledge available to us now, could only state that in some sense, the origin of life appears at the moment to be almost a miracle, so many are the conditions which would have had to have been satisfied to get it going."[38]

Statements like this could be multiplied a thousand times over. They show beyond a doubt that the best science by some of the most brilliant scientific minds leads us back, not to dead matter, but to a living God.

Mark Eastman, M.D., and Chuck Missler point out that when you boil down all the materialistic arguments for the origin of the universe, there are really just two options: 1) that matter is infinitely old (eternal), or 2) that matter appeared out of nothing at a finite point in the past. They point out, "There is no third option." These authors proceed to cite evidence to show that matter cannot be eternal, including evidence from physics, such as proton decay and evidence from the first and second laws of thermodynamics which "provide some of the strongest evidence for a finite universe."[39]

Almost everyone agrees that matter does exist, so we have to explain its existence somehow. If matter cannot be infinitely old— and the scientific evidence is so strong at this point as to make this conclusion inevitable—then our only option is that matter appeared in the universe out of nothing at a finite point in the past. Of course, if we begin with the "Big Bang" and an extremely small amount of dense matter, which has been dubbed the "cosmic egg" (it's less than the size of an atom according to some theorists), the problem is not yet solved. Where did such an "egg" originate? The origin of the alleged "cosmic egg" is a matter of intense debate, as well it should be. Either it existed forever (which is impossible) or it appeared on its own power out of nothing at a finite point in the past. The latter belief is not only unscientific and irrational, it is also impossible. Materialistically then, there is no explanation, nor will there be. And regardless, it requires a rather vivid imagination to think that something so hauntingly small (the size of a proton or electron, much smaller than an atom) could produce a universe as large as ours. How could something the size of an electron, of extremely dense "matter," through an explosion outward, produce the billions and *trillions* of ordered, complex galaxies in our universe, let alone all the intricacies of life? It's actually rather humorous, regardless of the size of the "egg." And what were the mechanisms that caused the supposed big bang? No one is saying with assurance because no one has any idea. The theories offered are simply the best that scientists can come up with, given what they have to work with. A universe exists, so they try to explain it.

Readers who want to dig deeper are encouraged to check their local Christian bookstore for books that offer a deeper examination of the validity of creation science versus the claims of evolution.

# THE UNIQUENESS OF CHRISTIANITY

### 6

## HOW DOES A PERSON FIND ONE TRUE GOD AMONG MANY?

*An honest man alters his ideas to fit the truth; a dishonest man alters the truth to fit his ideas.*

So far we have concluded that God does exist. If God exists, and assuming for now there is only one true God, how do we find Him? We find Him by a commitment to finding the truth based on the quality of the evidence. That's why this book is designed to take the reader through a succession of evidences that, we hope, will cause him or her to conclude there is truth and that it can both be known and experienced.

The difficulty is that all religions claim to be the truth (even scientific ones), and as a result, a lot of people are confused. Of course, not all religions can be fully true since they all clearly contradict one another. If all religions aren't true, either all are false or one is true. No other option is available. Any religion claiming that it alone is fully true and producing solid evidence to that effect is worth serious consideration for that reason alone. But only biblical Christianity does this. In fact, it may be said that from an evidential perspective, Christianity is actually superior to other worldviews, secular or religious, because it makes testable and verifiable claims.

Let us begin by examining some of the unique facts about Christianity that set it apart from other religions.

7
_____

## Is Christianity Unique when Compared with Other Religions, and Does It Matter?

One way to illustrate the uniqueness of Christianity is to evaluate different concepts of origins. In philosophical apologetics this approach was taken by the late Christian philosopher Dr. Francis Schaeffer in *He Is There and He Is Not Silent*. How do we attempt to explain our existence? Though there are hundreds of religions and philosophies, when they are reduced to their most common elements, they all share relatively few concepts of origins or explanations of reality:

1. The finite personal—creation by the gods

2. The infinite personal—creation by a God such as the Muslim Allah

3. The infinite impersonal monistic—e.g., creation (self-emanation) by the Brahman of Hinduism

4. The materialistic impersonal—creation by chance (evolution)

5. The infinite personal triune—creation by the God of the Bible.

Dr. Schaeffer's argument is essentially this: Only by beginning with the Christian view of origins can one adequately explain the universe as we know it in terms of metaphysics, epistemology, and morality. (Metaphysics deals with the nature of existence, truth, and knowledge; epistemology, with how we know; and morality, with how we should live.)

The problem with options one through four is that they cannot adequately explain and/or logically support these vital philosophical necessities. For example, in option one, the finite personal origin, the existence of mythical and bickering, capricious, and copulating finite gods (whether of the ancient Greeks and Romans or the modern Hindus and Buddhists) can't explain the nature of existence because they aren't big enough to create the world, let alone provide us with the infinite reference point we need in order to have absolute truth or to logically justify meaning in life. The preeminent atheist philosopher we discussed earlier, Jean Paul Sartre, was correct in stating that man required an infinite reference point in order for life to have any meaning. Since Sartre argued there was no such reference point, he stated, "Man is absurd, but he must grimly act as if he were not," and "Man is a useless passion."[40] On the other hand, the infinite personal triune God of the Bible is big enough to create the universe and big enough to provide man with an infinite reference point that gives his personal existence meaning. Amoral gods cannot provide any logical basis for moral living. But the God of the Bible, who is infinitely righteous, holy, and immutable, can provide such a basis.

The problem with option two, the infinite personal origin, is that such a God seems ultimately dependent upon his creation in order to express the attributes of his own nature and personality. In other words, for all eternity prior to creation, this God would have been alone with himself. With whom does He communicate? Whom does He love? (In part, this may explain why the absolute transcendence and "otherness" of the distant Muslim deity, Allah, is stressed so heavily in Islam and why Allah is not truly a God of love.)[41] It would appear that such a God is "forced" to create and is subsequently dependent upon his creation for expressing the attributes of his own personality—and is, therefore, not truly an independent or free divine Being. The concept of a God who is dependent on something else offers an inadequate conception of

God. The Christian view of origins solves this problem because the triune God (as Father, Son, and Holy Spirit) has no need to create in order to express His attributes of personality. The members of the Godhead communicate together and love one another for all eternity and are never dependent upon their creation for anything.

The problem with option three, the infinite, impersonal, monistic ("all is one") origin, is that it portrays a God who is infinite but impersonal, and therefore it gives no basis for explaining the origin of personality or any logical reason for personhood to have meaning. This explains why, in both Hinduism and Buddhism, the personality is seen as an "enemy" and is finally destroyed by absorption into Brahman or Nirvana. Not only the material creation but human existence, body and personality, are either an illusion as in Hinduism (*maya*), or so empty and impermanent as in Buddhism (*sunyata*), that they are ultimately meaningless. In the end, *man himself* is a hindrance to spiritual enlightenment and must be "destroyed" to find so-called "liberation." As Dr. Frits Staal comments in "Indian Concepts of the Body," "Whatever the alleged differences between Hindu and Buddhist doctrines, one conclusion follows from the preceding analysis. No features of the individual personality survive death in either state."[42] But is an impersonal "immortality" truly meaningful when it extinguishes our personal existence forever? Is it even desirable? As Sri Lankan Ajith Fernando, who has spoken to hundreds of Buddhists and Hindus, illustrates, "When I asked a girl who converted from Buddhism to Christianity through our ministry what attracted her to Christianity, the first thing she told me was, 'I did not want Nirvana.' The prospect of having all her desires snuffed out after a long and dreary climb [toward "liberation"] was not attractive to her."[43]

In addition, monistic philosophies provide no explanation for the diversity within creation. If "God is one," and the only reality, then diversity—all creation—is by definition part of the illusion of duality. That includes all morality, all human hopes and aspirations, and everything else that matters. In the end, despite having an infinite reference point, we are left with only a destructive nihilistic outlook on life. As Charles Manson noted, "If all is one, what is bad?" Indeed, Eastern Gurus frequently emphasize, often quite offensively, that life is unreal, meaningless, and finally worthless, which is why it must be denied and "transcended."[44]

The concept of an infinite personal triune God addresses these issues as well. Because God is personal, human personality has genuine and eternal significance. The only kind of eternity that has any meaning, or gives this life any meaning, is an eternity of personal immortality. And because Christianity involves a philosophy of religious dualism, God is the creator of a real creation. The creation is not simply the illusory emanation of an impersonal divine substance. As a result, there is no need to face the very destructive individual and public consequences of nihilism.

Option number four, the materialistic impersonal origin, has similar problems to option three—it is finally nihilistic, stripping our existence of any meaning. Ultimate reality is again impersonal, although not a divine substance. Ultimate reality is dead matter. There is no God, period. Where does anyone find any dignity or meaning when our own self-portrait is the cold atoms of deep space? In the end, in the words of philosopher Bertrand Russell, there is only "unyielding despair." After a single, probably difficult, life, we die forever. Although such a fate is infinitely more merciful than the endless reincarnations and final dissolutions of Hinduism and Buddhism, it is still far too nihilistic and despairing for most people to live out practically. As Leslie Paul observed, in this view, "All life is no more than a match struck in the dark and blown out again. The final result is to deprive it completely of meaning."[45]

Contrast the darkness of nihilistic theory with the unique doctrines of Christianity. Consider for example the Christian tenet of salvation.

If we break down the doctrine of salvation into its component parts,[46] we discover teachings that are found nowhere else in the world. How do we account for one religion that is unique theologically—not to mention evidentially, philosophically, and experientially—when all the other religions of the world teach nothing new? The common themes of other religions include salvation by works, philosophically compromised morality, polytheism, and occultism. Even Islam's monotheism was not unique. So how do we account for the development of completely unique teachings such as the Trinity, salvation entirely by grace, the doctrine of depravity and others, when they are still a mystery? If there was never a logical impetus for their initial development, how do we explain them apart from divine revelation?

Consider the doctrine of grace. Martin Luther, the great church reformer, once observed there are finally only two religions in the world: the religion of works and the religion of grace. Only biblical Christianity is a religion of grace because only biblical Christianity is a revelation from God.

All other religions we know of teach salvation by meritorious works. Christianity is the only religion that teaches salvation solely by grace through faith alone. (A few others claim it, but either the claim is invalid or the doctrine is not held in a Christian sense.) This simple fact makes Christianity stand entirely apart from other religions. It also necessitates an answer to the question, Why, out of the thousands of religions throughout history teaching salvation by works, is there only one religion teaching salvation by grace alone? Apart from divine revelation, how do we logically explain the origin of one religion that teaches something no other religion has ever taught? In other words, how did mankind acquire a religion of pure grace with salvation as a free gift when the human heart unyieldingly tends toward self-justifying works and self-earned salvation?

Again, the only satisfactory answer is divine revelation. This is exactly what the Bible claims. As the Apostle Paul emphasized: "I want you to know, brothers, that the gospel I preached is not something that man made up. I did not receive it from any man, nor was I taught it; rather, I received it by revelation from Jesus Christ" (Galatians 1:11-12). The gospel of Christianity is not something people made up because people never would have made it up; it goes against the grain of self-justification too sharply. The one true God personally revealed the one true way of salvation in the Bible. Obviously, He didn't reveal it in the scriptures of other religions because they contradict the Bible's most basic teachings, and God does not contradict Himself, nor is He a God of confusion (Titus 1:2; 1 Corinthians 14:33 NASB).

In sum, observers of religion and critics of Christianity must clarify why there is one religion of grace amidst universal religions of works. It seems the only explanation is that the one true God who exists is a God of grace (Ephesians 1:7; 2:6-9), and therefore, we find a single religion of grace among all that oppose it. Again, the same is true for the doctrine of the Trinity—no other religion, past or present, has such a doctrine of God, nor is such a doctrine likely to have been invented. The fact it is only found in Christianity makes the point.

In conclusion, the fact that Christianity more logically and adequately explains our existence than does any other religion, and that its theological teachings are unique, argue in part for biblical Christianity being the true religion.

---

### 8

### Is Jesus Unique when Compared with Other Religious Founders, and Does It Matter?

*The truth is always the strongest argument.*
**Sophocles**

In the words of an article in *Time* magazine, Christ's life was simply, "the most influential life that was ever lived."[47] It is difficult to ignore such a life.

Jesus said, "I am the truth" (John 14:6) and, "In fact, for this reason I was born, and for this I came into the world, to testify to the truth. Everyone on the side of truth listens to me" (John 18:37).

What if Jesus Christ's claim that *He* is the truth can be objectively determined to be valid by anyone who wishes to their own objective satisfaction?

Leading Christian philosopher Dr. Norman Geisler holds a Ph.D. in philosophy from Loyola University and has lectured or debated skeptics in 50 states and 25 countries on six continents. Among his 50-plus books are the impressive *Baker Encyclopedia of Christian Apologetics, When Critics Ask, When Skeptics Ask, In Defense of the Resurrection, Miracles and Modern Thought, Let Us Reason: an Introduction to Logical Thinking, Philosophy of Religion, Answering Islam,* and *Perspectives: Understanding and Evaluating Today's World Views.* As to Christian truth claims, he has probably researched every major competing religion and philosophy, and sharpened his thinking by debates with skeptics of all stripes. He concludes of Jesus: "Jesus Christ was unique in every way...Jesus stands above all other religious or moral teachers." And "Christ is absolutely unique among all who ever lived...He is unique in his supernatural nature, in his superlative character, and in his life and teaching...No other world teacher has claimed to be God. Even when the followers of some prophet deified their teacher, there is no proof given for that claim that can be compared to the fulfillment of prophecy, the sinless and miraculous life, and the resurrection...Jesus is absolutely unique among all human beings who ever lived."[48]

Most people don't think about the fact that Jesus achieved more than any other person in history, yet in only three years! By far those few years stimulated more commentary, literature, and general influence over 2000 years, than has the lifetime of anyone else. He was so unique that the religion begun by Him is the only world religion based entirely on a person, not a person's teachings. Any other religion can have their founder removed and the religion would survive and prosper. Remove Jesus from Christianity and it crumbles.

When we examine all the great religious teachers, leaders, founders, and prophets who have ever lived, who is the equal of

Jesus? No one. Neither Moses, Confucius, Buddha, nor Lao Tse (Taoism)—these never claimed to be anything other than sinful men. Neither Muhammad, Joseph Smith, Zoroaster, nor Guru Nanak (Sikhism)—ever gave any evidence they were true prophets of God. Neither Mahavira (Jainism), the leaders of Sufism (such as Jalal-ud-Din Rumi), nor the founder of any other religion the world has known has ever been like Jesus. There is even no other god that comes close to Jesus—neither the Allah of Islam, nor Brahman, Brahma, Vishnu, Shiva, or Krishna, the mythical, amoral deities of Hinduism, nor any other god comes close to the uniqueness, majesty, and love of Jesus. Neither animism, Buddhism, Confucianism, Hinduism, Islam, Jainism, Judaism, Mormonism, Shintoism, Sikhism, Sufism, Taoism, Zoroastrianism, nor any other religious belief outside Christianity has anyone who can even slightly be compared to Jesus. We suggest the reader perform his or her own study on the matter.

If we examine the specific claims of the founders of the great religions, we find none of them claims and does what Jesus does. In terms of influence, Muhammad and Buddha are the only distant competitors with Jesus. But the differences are vast. In the Koran the Muslim prophet Muhammad states, "Muhammad is naught but a messenger" and "Surely I am no more than a human apostle."[49] In fact, several times in the Koran, Muhammad is acknowledged as sinful, asks forgiveness from God, or is even rebuked by God.[50] Muhammad confessed he was sinful; Jesus claimed He was sinless. Muhammad only claimed to be a prophet of God; Jesus claimed to be God. Muhammad was rebuked by God; Jesus was never rebuked by God. In fact, He said, "I always do what pleases him" (John 8:29).

The difference between the two could not be more pronounced:

> Muhammad was a prophet of conquest and war who took life by force;
> Jesus is the Prince of Peace who gives life by faith.

Muhammad shed others' blood for Islam;
Jesus shed His own blood for others.

Muhammad is in his tomb;
Jesus is not.

Muhammad said the witness of a woman was half the value of the witness of a man and that husbands can beat their wives for disobedience;
Jesus honored women and taught that a husband is to love his wife as sacrificially as He loved the church.

Muhammad taught God is unlimited power;
Jesus taught God is undiminished love.

Muhammad promoted persecution against "infidels" and constrained people by conquest;
Jesus forgives "infidels," taught "love your enemies," and constrains people by love.

Rejecting Muhammad's teachings makes believers peace-loving.
Accepting Jesus' teachings makes believers peace loving.

Muhammad allowed that a cleric of Islam could be a terrorist;
Jesus requires that a pastor in the church be above reproach.

Muhammad wanted to conquer the world for Islam;
Christ wants to change the world for God's glory.

Muhammad persecuted Jews even to death;
Christ ordered that the gospel be preached "to the Jew first."

Muhammad's teachings led to the belief that those who leave Islam are to be killed;
Jesus taught that those who choose to leave the church are allowed to do so freely.

Muhammad's teachings have led to great persecution, even slaughter, of Christians for 1400 years and to expansion of the faith by force;
Jesus' teachings have led to great compassion and mercy to Muslims for 1400 years and to expansion of the faith by love.[51]

Consider the Buddha. Buddhism, a nihilistic religion, is increasingly popular in the West and is itself a symptom of the decay of Western culture. The Buddha simply claimed to be an "enlightened" man, one who could show others how to escape the futility of this world and find eternal release from suffering in a state of individual nonexistence called "nirvana." After his alleged enlightenment, the Buddha said he realized the importance of maintaining an attitude of equanimity toward all things because this attitude helps one to end the cycle of rebirth, attain permanent release from the human condition, and "enter" nirvana:

> Monks, I'm a Brahmana [enlightened being], one to ask a favor of, ever clean-handed, wearing my last body. I am inexorable, bear no love nor hatred toward anyone. I have the same feelings for respectable people as for the low; for moral persons as for the immoral; for the depraved as for those who observe the rules of good conduct. You disciples do not affirm that the Lord Buddha reflects thus within himself, "I bring salvation to every living being." Subhuti entertain no such delusive thought! Because in reality there are no living beings to whom the Lord Buddha can bring salvation.[52]

Noted professor of religion Houston Smith comments about the Buddha in *The Religions of Man*: "Notwithstanding his own objectivity toward himself, there was constant pressure during his lifetime to turn him into a god. He rebuffed all these categorically, insisting that he was human in every respect. He made no attempt to conceal his temptations and weaknesses, how difficult it had been to attain enlightenment, how narrow the margin by which he had won through, how fallible he still remained."[53]

Clive Erricker, a lecturer and prolific writer in the field of religious studies with a special interest in Buddhism, writes of the Buddha in *Buddhism*, "Indeed, he did not even claim that his teachings were a unique and original source of wisdom...[citing John Bowker, *Worlds of Faith* (London: Ariel Books, 1983)]. Buddha always said, 'Don't take what I'm saying [on my own authority], just try to analyze as far as possible and see whether what I'm saying makes sense or not. If it doesn't make sense, discard it. If it does make sense, then pick it up.'"[54]

Buddha claimed merely a personal "enlightenment" designed to escape being human; Jesus claimed (in His own nature) to be the Light of the world. Buddha claimed it was wrong to consider him one who brings salvation to men because men, having no permanent reality, do not finally exist; Jesus taught that He came to bring salvation to all men and to dignify their existence eternally. The Buddha promised to give others "enlightenment" so that they might find nirvana, a state of personal dissolution in the afterlife; Jesus promised to give men abundant life and personal immortality in heaven forever. Buddha had the same feelings for good and evil; Jesus exalted righteousness and hated evil.

Confucius said, "As to being a Divine Sage or even a Good Man, far be it from me to make any such claim."[55] Confucius denied that he was divine or even a good man; Jesus claimed He was divine and morally perfect. Zoroaster only claimed to be a prophet, "I was ordained by Thee at the first. All others I look upon with hatred of spirit."[56] Lao-Tse and Guru Nanak sum up the attitude, at one time or another, of all the great religious founders when they confessed their humanity and even their ignorance. For example, Lao-Tse, the founder of Taoism, said, "I alone appear empty. Ignorant am I, O so ignorant! I am dull! I alone am confused, so confused!"[57] Even in the latter part of his life, Guru Nanak, the founder of Sikhism, still struggled to achieve enlightenment and lamented over his own spiritual darkness: "I have become perplexed in my search. In the darkness I find no way. Devoted to pride, I weep in sorrow. How shall deliverance be obtained?"[58]

In *The World's Living Religions*, professor of the history of religions Robert Hume comments that there are three features of Christian faith that "cannot be paralleled anywhere among the religions of the world."[59] These include the character of God as a loving heavenly Father, the character of the founder of Christianity as the Son of God, and the work of the Holy Spirit. Further,

All of the nine founders of religion, with the exception of Jesus Christ, are reported in their respective sacred scriptures as having passed through a preliminary period of uncertainty, or of searching for religious light. All the founders of the non-Christian religions evinced inconsistencies in their personal character; some of them altered their practical policies under change of circumstances. Jesus Christ alone is reported as having had a consistent God-consciousness, a consistent character himself, and a consistent program for his religion.[60]

If the claims of religious leaders mean anything, and certainly they must, whether true or false, then no one else in history ever claimed and did what Jesus did. He says, "I am the light of the world. Whoever follows me will never walk in darkness, but will have the light of life" (John 8:12). How many other men ever said such a thing? Jesus claimed, "I am the way, the truth and the life. No one comes to the Father except through Me" (John 14:6). How many other men ever claimed that? Jesus even claimed that 1500 years before His birth, Moses wrote about Him, and further that the entire Old Testament, from 1500–400 B.C., bore witness to *Him* (John 5:46-47; Luke 24:27, 44).

Jesus commanded men to love Him in exactly the same way that they love God—with all their heart, soul, and mind (Matthew 22:37-38). Jesus said that God the Holy Spirit would bear witness of Him and glorify Him (John 16:14). Who ever made such a claim? Jesus said that to know Him was to know God (John 14:7). To receive Him was to receive God (Matthew 10:40). To honor Him was to honor God (John 5:23). To believe in Him was to believe in God (John 12:44-45; 14:1). To see Him was to see God (John 8:19; 14:7). To deny Him was to deny God (1 John 2:23). To hate Him was to hate God (John 15:23). Did any other religious founder in history ever make such statements?

In Mark 2:10-11, Jesus claimed He could forgive sins—something all religions concede is reserved to God alone. In John 10:28 and 11:25, He said He could give all who believed in Him eternal life. How can a mere man, indeed anyone less than God, give eternal life to creatures who die? Yet Jesus raised the dead even in front of His critics and enemies—not in some dark alley, but before scores of eyewitnesses (Luke 7:11-15; 8:41-42, 49-56; John 11:43-44). Who ever did *that*? He did other miracles that amazed those who saw them: "Nobody has ever heard of opening the eyes of a man born blind" (John 9:32). "We have never seen anything like this!" (Mark 2:12).

In Matthew 25, Jesus said that He will actually return at the end of the world, that He Himself will judge every person who ever lived, that He will personally raise all the dead of history, and that all the nations will be gathered before Him. He will sit on His throne of glory and judge and separate men from one another as a shepherd does the sheep from the goats (Matthew 25:31-46, see also John 5:25-34). Just as clearly, Jesus taught that every person's eternal destiny depends upon how they treat Him (John 8:24; Matthew 10:32). Again, who has ever made such claims? All these statements and many more like them leave us little choice. Either Jesus is who He said He is—God incarnate—or else He was absolutely mad. But who can believe *that*?

Christianity's unique impact, teachings, and founder are startling testimonies to its truth, and would thus probably be the best place to start a search for absolute truth in religion. But its uniqueness does not prove Christianity is the one true religion. Hard evidence is needed for that. And if only one religion is true, it must be hard evidence that is not found in any other religion.

---

## 9

## IS THE EVIDENCE FOR CHRISTIANITY WORTH INVESTIGATING?

We have just seen that among the religions of the world, Christianity is unique in many ways. And the evidence supporting its claims are *testable*. This too is unique. As trial lawyer, philosopher, and theologian Dr. John Warwick Montgomery points out, "The historic Christian claim differs qualitatively from the claims of all other world religions at the epistemological point: on the issue of testability."[61] In other words, only Christianity stakes its claim to truthfulness on historical events open to critical investigation. This explains the number of conversions by skeptics throughout history, who, having examined the evidence critically, even trying their best to disprove it, nevertheless became Christians. For example, Viggo Olsen, M.D., author of *Daktar: Diplomat in Bangladesh,* and his wife were both skeptics who "decided to embark on a detailed study of Christianity with the intention of rejecting it on intellectual grounds. Little by little, as they studied works that deal with data common to apologetics and evidences...they were led step by step to see the truthfulness of Christianity. Their study was no minor investigation or casual perusal. It was an exhaustive search...."[62]

If Christianity were "obviously" false, as some skeptics charge, the esteemed intellectuals cited below could not logically make the following declarations about the truth of Christianity. The fact that they do suggests something of great import for relativists. While testimonies per se mean little, if they are corroborated by the weight of concrete evidence, they can hardly be dismissed. Collectively, testimonies like these present a weight of support that cannot be ignored. For these men are not fools, nor are they ignorant, but include many prominent academics, philosophers, intellectuals, scholars, and researchers who have made critical examinations of detailed houses of evidence. Mortimer Adler is one of the world's leading philosophers, chairman of the board of editors for *The Encyclopædia Britannica,* architect of *The Great Books of the Western World* series and its remarkable *Syntopicon,* director of the prestigious Institute for Philosophical Research in Chicago, and author of many challenging books. He simply asserts, "I believe Christianity is the only logical, consistent faith in the world."[63] How could Adler make such a statement? He knows it can't rationally be made of any other religion.

The individual widely considered to be the greatest Protestant philosopher of God in the world, Alvin Plantinga, recalls, "For nearly my entire life I have been convinced of the truth of Christianity."[64] On what basis can one of the world's greatest philosophers make such a declaration if the evidence for Christianity is unconvincing, as many critics charge?

Dr. Drew Trotter is executive director of the Center for Christian Studies at Charlottesville, Virginia. He holds a doctorate from Cambridge University and argues convincingly that "logic and the evidence both point to the reality of absolute truth, and that truth is revealed in Christ."[65]

George F. Gilder may go down in history as one of its great minds. Technological visionary, noted economist and sociologist, and author of *Wealth and Poverty* and *Telecosm,* he asserts, "Christianity is true, and its truth will be discovered anywhere you look very far."[66]

Alister McGrath, principal of Wycliffe Hall, Oxford University, and author of *Intellectuals Don't Need God and Other Myths,* declares that the superior nature of the evidence for Christianity is akin to that found in doing good scientific research: "When I was undertaking my doctoral research in molecular biology at Oxford University, I was frequently confronted with a number of theories offering to explain a given observation. In the end, I had to make a judgment concerning which of them possessed the greatest internal consistency, the greatest degree of correspondence to the data of empirical observation, and the greatest degree of predictive ability. Unless I was to abandon any possibility of advance in understanding, I was obliged to make such a judgment...I would claim the right to speak of the 'superiority' of Christianity in this explicative sense."[67]

The noted Christian scholar Dr. Carl F.H. Henry wrote a three-thousand-page, six-volume work on the topic of *God, Revelation and Authority.* After his exhaustive analysis, Henry declared, "Truth is Christianity's most enduring asset...."[68]

Dr. Robert A. Morey writes, "There is more than enough evidence on every hand from every department of human experience and knowledge to demonstrate that Christianity is true...[It is] the faith of the non-Christian [that] is externally and internally groundless. They are the ones who leap in the dark. Some, like Kierkegaard, have admitted this."[69]

Such accolades could be multiplied repeatedly, and they are not made lightly. Again men like these aren't idiots. James Sire correctly points out in *Why Should Anyone Believe Anything at All?* that an argument for belief, religious or other, must be secured on the best evidence, validly argued, and able to refute the strongest objections that can be mustered against it.[70] To be sure, as Dr. Norman Geisler comments, "In the face of overwhelming apologetic evidence, unbelief becomes perverse...."[71]

Obviously, if the God of the Bible has revealed Himself and if He is the only true God—and if Christ is the only way of salvation—then we would expect good evidence. Not just some evidence, or inferior evidence, but superior evidence. As Dr. Montgomery asks:

> What if a revelational truth-claim did not turn on questions of theology and religious philosophy—on any kind of esoteric, fideistic method available only to those who are already "true believers"—but on the very reasoning employed in the law to determine questions of fact?... Eastern faiths and Islam, to take familiar examples, ask the uncommitted seeker to discover their truth experientially: the faith-experience will be self-validating...Christianity, on the other hand, declares that the truth of its absolute claims rests squarely on certain historical facts, open to ordinary investigation...The advantage of a jurisprudential approach lies in the difficulty of jettisoning it: legal standards of evidence developed as essential means of resolving the most intractable disputes in society...Thus one cannot very well throw out legal reasoning merely because its application to Christianity results in a verdict for the Christian faith.[72]

Further, when one examines all the arguments and attacks made *against* Christianity for 2000 years by some of the greatest minds on the other side, one only finds that individually or collectively, they do not disprove Christianity. But they do negate other religions—Islam, Hinduism, Buddhism, etc. These religions can also be tested by examining their claims and looking critically at the facts—but again, one finds they are invalidated by such a procedure. What is characteristically if unfortunately overlooked in the field of comparative religion today is the issue of truth— and that no genuinely historical or objective evidence exists for the foundational claims of Hinduism, Buddhism, Islam, or any other world religion.[73]

Indeed, other religions in the world are believed despite the lack of valid evidence supporting their truth claims; only Christianity can claim credibility *because* of such evidence. Subjective experience, blind faith, tradition, and opinion, may be comforting, but they prove little. If there is only one God and if only one religion is fully true, then one should not expect to discover sustainable evidence in any other religion.

Only Christianity meets the burden of proof necessary to say, This religion alone is fully true. That means Jesus Christ really is the only way of salvation because no one can argue successfully that Christianity has not been thoroughly investigated and tested. As the fifth edition of *Man's Religions* by John B. Noss points out, "The first Christian century has had more books written about it than any other comparable period of history. The chief sources bearing on its history are the gospels and epistles of the New Testament, and these—again we must make a comparative statement—have been more thoroughly searched by inquiring minds than any other books ever written."[74]

Now we are ready to assess the evidence that actually proves Christianity is the one true religion. We clearly cannot discuss all the evidence, but we can discuss enough to make the point. "Evidence" is defined in the *Oxford American Dictionary* as "1. anything that establishes a fact or gives reason for believing something.

2. statements made or objects produced in a law court as proof or to support a case." We will use the sense of both definitions. "Proof" is defined as "1. a fact or thing that shows or helps to show that something is true or exists. 2. a demonstration of the truth of something. 3. the process of testing whether something is true or good or valid..." We will use all three definitions.

Let us begin with the primary source documents. We will show there is no reason to doubt the textual and historical accuracy of the Bible, even its specific details. Given its age (2000–3500 years), large number of books (66) and authors (40-plus), and the fact that it was written over a period of some 1500 years, this is a striking conclusion.

---

10

---

## CAN WE KNOW THE NEW TESTAMENT DOCUMENTS ARE TRUSTWORTHY?

*There is, I imagine, no body of literature in the world that has been exposed to the stringent analytical study that the four gospels have sustained for the past 200 years...scholars today who treat the gospels as credible historical documents do so in the full light of this analytical study.*

F. F. Bruce

Skeptical non-Christians, including members of other religions like Islam and Mormonism, are distrustful of the credibility of the Gospels and the other New Testament documents. For the Christian, few things are more critical than the words of Jesus, who assured his followers, "Heaven and earth will pass away, but my words will never pass away" (Matthew 24:35). Jesus' promise is of no small import. If His words were not accurately recorded, how can anyone know what He really taught? The truth is, we couldn't know. Further, if the remainder of the New Testament cannot be established to be historically reliable, then little can be known about what true Christianity really is, teaches, or means.

Christians argue that the New Testament text is reliable history in spite of the novel and sometimes ingenious speculations of critics who, while often familiar with the facts, refuse to accept them due to preexisting bias. The methods used by the critics (including rationalistic higher critical methods such as source and form criticism) claim "assured results" that prove Scripture unreliable. But these methods have been weighed in the balance of *secular* scholarship and found defective. Their use in biblical analysis to declare the text unreliable is therefore unjustified. The positive fruit they have borne is minuscule, and negatively, they are responsible for confusing people about biblical authority and destroying their confidence in the Bible.

The honesty and accuracy of the New Testament writers is established, and no critic can logically deny it. Paul Barrett's *Is the New Testament Reliable?* and Craig Blomberg's *The Historical Reliability of the Gospels* are two of many texts that demonstrate this.

The following ten facts allow us to prove the trustworthiness of the New Testament.

To begin, the historical accuracy of the New Testament can be proven by subjecting it to three generally accepted tests for determining historical reliability. Such tests are utilized in literary criticism and the study of historical documents in general.[75] These are the 1) bibliographical, 2) internal, and 3) external tests of historical evidence.

### The Bibliographical Test (corroboration from textual transmission)

The bibliographical test seeks to determine if we can reconstruct the original New Testament writings from the extant copies at hand. We have 5300 Greek manuscripts and manuscript portions, 10,000 Latin Vulgate, and 9300 other versions—plus 36,000 early (100–300 A.D.) patristic quotations of the New Testament—so that all but a few verses of the entire text could be reconstructed from these alone.[76] (There are 19,368 citations from the Gospels alone.)[77]

Few scholars question the general reliability of ancient classical literature on the basis of the manuscripts we possess. Yet this manuscript evidence is vastly inferior to that of the New Testament. For example, of 16 well-known classical authors (Plutarch, Tacitus, Seutonius, Polybius, Thucydides, Xenophon, and others), the total number of extant copies is typically less than ten, and the earliest copies date from 750 to 1600 years after the original manuscript was first penned.[78] We need only compare such slim evidence to the mass of biblical documentation involving over 24,000 manuscript portions, manuscripts, and versions, the earliest fragment and complete copies dating between 50 and 300 years after the originals were written.

Given the fact that the early Greek manuscripts (the Papyri and early Uncials) date much closer to the originals than do the earliest manuscripts of other ancient literature, and the overwhelming additional abundance of manuscript attestation, any doubt as to the integrity or authenticity of the New Testament text has been removed. Indeed, this kind of evidence is the dream of the historian. No other ancient literature has ever come close to supplying historians and textual critics with such an abundance of data. The late Dr. F.F. Bruce, former Ryland's Professor of Biblical Criticism and Exegesis at the University of Manchester, asserted of the New Testament: "There is no body of ancient literature in the world which enjoys such a wealth of good textual attestation as the New Testament."[79] Professor Bruce further commented, "The evidence for our New Testament writings is ever so much greater than the evidence for many writings of classical writers, the authenticity of which no one dreams of questioning. And if the New Testament were a collection of secular writings, their authenticity would generally be regarded as beyond all doubt."[80]

It is this wealth of material that has enabled scholars such as Westcott and Hort, Ezra Abbott, Philip Schaff, A.T. Robertson, Norman Geisler, and William Nix to place the restoration of the original text at better than 99 percent.[81] Hort's estimate of "substantial variation" for the New Testament is one-tenth of one percent, Abbott's estimate is one-fourth of one percent, and even

Hort's figure including trivial variation is less than 2 percent. Sir Frederic Kenyon well summarizes the situation:

> The number of manuscripts of the New Testament…is so large that it is practically certain that the true reading of every doubtful passage is preserved in some one or another of these ancient authorities. This can be said of no other ancient book in the world. Scholars are satisfied that they possess substantially the true text of the principal Greek and Roman writers whose works have come down to us, of Sophocles, of Thucydides, of Cicero, of Virgil; yet our knowledge depends on a mere handful of manuscripts, whereas the manuscripts of the New Testament are counted by hundreds and even thousands.[82]

In other words, those who question the reliability of the New Testament must also question the reliability of virtually every ancient writing the world possesses! How can the Bible be rejected when its documentation is literally more than one hundred times more substantial than that of other ancient literature? Because it is impossible to question the world's ancient classics, it is far more impossible to question the reliability of the New Testament.[83] To do so is to throw out history and close down many university departments.

## The Internal Evidence Test (corroboration from content accuracy)

This test asserts that one is to assume the truthful reporting of an ancient document, and not assume either fraud, incompetence or error, unless the author of the document has disqualified himself by their presence. For example, do the New Testament writers contradict themselves? Is there anything in their writing that causes one to suspect their trustworthiness? Are there statements or assertions in the text which are demonstrably false according to known archæological, historic, or scientific data?

The answer is no. There is lack of proven fraud or error on the part of any New Testament writer. But there is consistent evidence of careful eyewitness reporting. The caution exercised by the writers, their personal conviction that what they wrote was true, and the lack of demonstrable error or contradiction indicate that the Gospel authors and, indeed, all the New Testament authors pass the second test as well (Luke 1:1-4; John 19:35; 21:24; Acts 1:1-3; 2:22; 26:24-26; 2 Peter 1:16; 1 John 1:1-3).

For example, the kinds of details the Gospel writers include in their narratives offer strong evidence for their integrity. They record their own sins and failures, even serious ones (Matthew 26:56, 72-75; Mark 10:35-45). They do not hesitate to accurately record even the most difficult and consequential statements of Jesus (John 6:41-71). They forthrightly supply the embarrassing and even capital charges of Jesus' own enemies. Thus, even though Jesus was their very Messiah and Lord, they not only record the charges that Jesus broke the Sabbath, but that He was born in fornication, a blasphemer and a liar, insane, and even demonized (see Matthew 1:19, 26:65; John 7:20,48; 8:41,48,52; 10:20,33, etc.)! To encounter such honesty in reporting incidents of this nature gives one assurance that the Gospel writers placed a very high premium on truthfulness. If they did not feel free to omit material that was embarrassing or controversial, is it logical to assume they distorted and invented material they knew was false? It's not likely. Consider also the manner in which the Gospels and rest of the New Testament are written—in contrast to the mythology and carelessness of much ancient writing, they are restrained and conscientious, "with accurate incidental details, with obvious care and exactitude."[84]

## The External Evidence Test (corroboration from reliable sources outside the New Testament)

The test of external evidence compares the documents with additional historical literature and data. Is there corroborating evidence outside the Bible for the claims made in the Gospels? Or are the claims of the New Testament successfully refuted by other competent reports or eyewitnesses? Any honest investigation will reveal that the New Testament passes the test. For example, the resurrection itself was never refuted, even by Jesus' own enemies.

Papias, a student of the Apostle John[85] and Bishop of Hierapolis around 130 A.D., observed that the Apostle John himself noted that Mark, in writing his Gospel, "wrote down accurately ...whatsoever [Peter] remembered of the things said or done by Christ. Mark committed no error ...for he was careful of one thing, not to omit any of the things [Peter] had heard, and not to state any of them falsely."[86] Fragments of Papias' *Exposition of the Oracles of the Lord,* written around 140 A.D., assert that the Gospels of Matthew, Mark, and John are all based on reliable eyewitness testimony (his portion on Luke is missing).[87] In his book *The Verdict of History,* Dr. Gary Habermas discusses 39 ancient sources which refer to over one hundred facts concerning Jesus' life teachings and resurrection; 24, including seven secular accounts, refer to His divine nature.[88]

Thus the relevant bibliographic, internal, and external evidence forces us to concede the historical accuracy and reliability of the Gospel and other New Testament accounts. The Scriptures pass persuasive tests which determine their integrity. Even two hundred years of recent scholarly rationalistic biblical criticism have proven nothing except that the writers were careful and honest reporters of the events recorded, and that the methods attempting to discredit them were flawed and biased from the start.[89] (The same assessment as to reliability can be demonstrated for the entire Old Testament as well.)[90]

In conclusion, these three tests tell us that it is not only a demonstrable historical fact that Jesus lived and taught what the New Testament says He lived and taught, but it is also a fact that the New Testament is the best-documented and most accurately preserved book of ancient history. In the words of Dr. Geisler, "To reject the historicity of the New Testament is to reject all history."[91] No one can reject all of history, no matter how much faith they have. That means we can trust what the New Testament authors say is true. For example, when we examine the evidence for something like the resurrection of Jesus as reported in the New Testament, there is no logical, historical, or other basis upon which to doubt what is written. Of course, if Jesus did rise from the dead as proof of His claims, the implications are momentous.

## Corroboration from Non-Christian Sources

The existence of both Jewish and secular accounts, to a significant degree, confirm the broad picture of Christ we have in the New Testament.[92] For example, scholarly research, such as that by Dr. Gary Habermas in *Ancient Evidence for the Life of Jesus* and other works, indicates that "a broad outline of the life of Jesus" and His death by crucifixion can be reasonably and directly inferred from entirely non-Christian sources.[93] Even the resurrection of Christ can be indirectly inferred.[94] New Testament authority Dr. Craig Blomberg points out that ancient historians generally dealt with leading figures and major philosophical movements, yet the amount that we can learn about Jesus from non-Christian sources that confirm key events and teachings in His life is remarkable, considering those events and teachings fit none of the basic categories ancient historians would write upon.[95]

## Corroboration from Enemies' Silence

The fact that so many people had extremely good reasons to discredit Christianity from the start and yet were unable to do so speaks volumes. All that the enemies of Jesus and the church had to do to disprove His claim to be the Messiah was to show that He did not fulfill messianic prophecies. To discredit the resurrection, they simply needed to produce His body. The fact that those who opposed the Gospel could not disprove it testifies to its truth.

## Corroboration from Eyewitnesses

The presence of hundreds of eyewitnesses to the events recorded in the New Testament would surely have prohibited any alteration or distortion of the facts, just as today any false reporting of specific events of the Vietnam War or World War II would be corrected on the basis of living eyewitnesses and historic records.

Some argue that the Gospel writers' reporting of miracle events can't be trusted because they were only giving their religiously excited "subjective experience" of Jesus, not objectively reporting real events. They thought Jesus did miracles, but were mistaken. What is ignored by critics is their own bias against miracles and what the text plainly states. The writers emphasized they were literally eyewitnesses of the nature and deeds of Jesus (Luke 1:2; Acts 2:32; 2 Peter 1:16), and they said that their testimony should be believed because it was true (John 20:30-31). These eyewitnesses claimed the miracles were done openly before multitudes, skeptics and believers alike. They were not done in a corner or some dark alley (Acts 26:26).

The apostles wrote that Jesus Himself presented His miracles in support of His claims to be both the prophesied Messiah and God incarnate. In Mark 2:8-11 when He healed the paralytic, He did so "that you may know that the Son of Man has authority on earth to forgive sins"—a clear claim to being God. In John 10:33, the Jews accused Jesus of blaspheming because He was claiming to be God. What was Christ's response? "Do not believe me unless I do what my Father does. But if I do it, even though you do not believe me, believe the miracles, that you may learn and understand that the Father is in me, and I in the Father" (John 10:37-38).

The teachings and miracles of Jesus, as any objective reading of the Gospels will show, are so inexorably bound together that if one removes the miracles, one must also discard the teachings. It is logically impossible to have any other Jesus than the biblical one. But it is precisely the biblical Jesus—His deeds and teaching—who has such abundant eyewitness testimony, as again, any reading of the Gospels and Acts will show.

## Corroboration from Date of Authorship

The fact that both conservatives (F. F. Bruce, John Wenham) and liberals (Bishop John A.T. Robinson) have penned defenses of early dating for the New Testament is a witness to the strength of the data on its behalf. The Gospels are extremely close to the events which they record. The first three can be dated as early as 10 to 25 years from the events cited, and this may also be true for the fourth Gospel. Regardless, all four Gospels were written well within the lifetimes of eyewitnesses, so that abundant opportunity existed for those with contrary evidence to examine the witnesses and refute them.

In *Redating Matthew, Mark and Luke,* noted conservative British scholar John Wenham presents a convincing argument that the synoptic Gospels are to be dated before 55 A.D. He dates Matthew at 40 A.D. (some tradition says the early 30s), Mark at 45 A.D., and Luke no later than 51–55 A.D.[96]

The late liberal bishop John A.T. Robinson began *Redating the New Testament* as what he labeled "a theological joke": "I thought I would see how far one could get with the hypothesis that the whole of the New Testament was written before 70." To his great surprise, he concluded that the entire New Testament was written and in circulation between 40 and 65 A.D., with the Gospel of John as early as before 40 A.D.[97] Indeed, it is becoming an increasingly persuasive argument that all the New Testament books were written before 70 A.D.—within a single generation of the death of Christ.

The implications of this are hardly small. A New Testament written before 70 A.D. virtually destroys the premises of higher criticism. There wasn't enough time for the early church to embellish the records with their own particularist views. So, what the New Testament reports, it reports accurately.

## Corroboration from Critical Methods Themselves

Even the critical methods themselves, such as source, form, and redaction criticism indirectly support New Testament reliability. Although higher critical theories in general reject biblical reliability, nevertheless, when such theories "are subjected to the same analytical scrutiny as they apply to the New Testament documents, they will be found to make their own contribution to validating the historicity of those records."[98] If 200 years of higher criticism of the biblical text reveals anything, it is that the higher critical methods are untrustworthy, not the Bible. And they have been discredited for at least as long. To illustrate, Richard Whately (1787–1863) of Oxford University held a seat in the House of Commons and wrote *Elements of Rhetoric*, which still exerts influence today in colleges in North America and Europe. In "Historic Doubts Relative to Napoleon Bonaparte," a logical satire upon historical skepticism, Whately dissects David Hume's theories regarding the validity of the Gospels by applying them to the existence of Napoleon Bonaparte, proving that Napoleon could not have lived as a single, identifiable individual, but was probably at least a composite and perhaps entirely mythical. He shows that if the French can believe in Napoleon, then by applying Hume's critical methods, "such a people must be prepared to believe anything. They might fancy their own country to abound not only with Napoleons but with dragons and centaurs and 'men whose heads do grow beneath their shoulders' or anything else that any lunatic ever dreamed of. If we could suppose the French capable of such monstrous credulity as the above supposition would imply, it is plain their testimony must be altogether worthless."[99] What "Historic Doubts" did to the liberal critics' views of Christ, Whately's "Historic Certainties Respecting the Early History of America" did to the liberal critics' skepticism about the reliability of the Bible in general.

## Corroboration from Legal Testimony and Former Skeptics

The evidence we have discussed as to the reliability of the New Testament explains why many intellectuals and former skeptics from all walks of life and professions agree the New Testament is trustworthy. Dr. Blomberg points out, "…there are plenty of stories of scholars in the New Testament field who have not been Christians, yet through their study of these very issues have come to faith in Christ."[100] In addition, many great minds of legal history have, on the grounds of strict evidence alone, accepted the

New Testament as accurate history, even with its miracles. For example, "The competence of the New Testament documents would be established in any court of law."[101] Simon Greenleaf was one of the greatest authorities on common-law evidence in Western history. In his book *Testimony of the Evangelists Examined by the Rules of Evidence Administered in Courts of Justice*, he powerfully demonstrated the reliability of the Gospels.[102]

Edmund H. Bennett (1824–1898), for over 20 years the dean of Boston University Law School, likewise penned *The Four Gospels from a Lawyer's Standpoint* (1899).[103] Irwin Linton, who had represented cases before the Supreme Court, wrote *A Lawyer Examines the Bible*, in which he stated,

> So invariable had been my observation that he who does not accept wholeheartedly the evangelical, conservative belief in Christ and the Scriptures has never read, has forgotten, or never been able to weigh—and certainly is utterly unable to refute—the irresistible force of the cumulative evidence upon which such faith rests, that there seems ample ground, for the conclusion that such ignorance is an invariable element in such unbelief. And this is so even though the unbeliever be a preacher, who is supposed to know this subject if he knows no other.[104]

There are also hundreds of contemporary lawyers who, also on the grounds of strict legal evidence, accept the New Testament as historically accurate. Sir Norman Anderson lectured at Princeton University, was offered a professorship for life at Harvard University, and was dean of the Faculty of Laws at the University of London. He is one of the greatest authorities on Islamic law, but a Christian by persuasion, fully convinced of New Testament authority and reliability, as argued in *Christianity: the Witness of History*. The eminent Lord Chancellor Hailsham has twice held the highest office possible for a lawyer in England, that of Lord Chancellor. He wrote "The Door Wherein I Went," in which he upholds the truth of the Christian religion.[105]

The burden for proving otherwise rests with the critic, who in 2000 years has yet to make a case. Even if we personally choose to disbelieve what the New Testament teaches, our disbelief changes nothing. Jesus Christ is who the New Testament says He is.

# THE BIBLE AS TRUTH

## 11

### WHY IS BIBLICAL PROPHECY IMPORTANT?

*I have examined whether this God has not left some sign of Himself. I see many contradictory religions, and consequently all false save one. Each wants to be believed on its own authority, and threatens unbelievers. I do not therefore believe them. Every one can say this; every one can call himself a prophet. But I see that Christian religion wherein prophecies are fulfilled; and that is what every one cannot do.*

**Blaise Pascal**

One of the strongest evidences of the divine inspiration of the Bible is the testimony of fulfilled prophecy. In world literature, the Bible is unique in this respect. At best, other religions' scriptures contain a small number of vague predictions, or their predictions fail, but nothing anywhere is comparable to the large number of detailed prophecies in Scripture.

Those who seriously examine biblical prophecy will quickly discover the subject of prophecy is not something rare or occasional in the pages of Scripture. There are more than 600 direct references in the Bible to "prophecy" and "prophets." An incredible 27 percent of the entire Bible contains prophetic material, most of which has already come true and some that remains to be fulfilled. Only four of the 66 books of the Bible are without prophecy—Ruth, the Song of Solomon, Philemon, and 3 John.[106] Even the shortest book of the Bible mentions prophecy (Jude 14, 17-18). The Apostle Peter tells us that we "will do well to pay attention to it" because biblical prophecy is not the words of men, nor the interpretations of men, but the words and interpretation of God (2 Peter 1:19-21). Jesus even rebuked His own disciples for ignoring it: "How foolish you are, and how slow of heart to believe all that the prophets have spoken!" (Luke 24:25). In addition, Jesus taught that Old Testament predictions concerning Himself were of special importance. He said, "This is what I told you while I was still with you: Everything must be fulfilled that is written about me in the Law of Moses, the Prophets and the Psalms" (Luke 24:44, see also verse 27; Matthew 5:17; John 5:39). Here and elsewhere, Jesus taught that the entire Hebrew Bible was about *Him*—that 39 separate books written by 30 different authors over a period of 1000 years, from 1500 to 400 B.C., predicted the events of *His* life in particular detail!

To be sure, prophecy is important because the *entire* Bible is Christological: "Jesus Christ remains the heart of prophecy."[107] In a fascinating study, *Christ: The Theme of the Bible*, Dr. Norman Geisler concludes that Christ is present in all 66 books of the Bible, even though 39 were written before He was born. Christ fulfills literally dozens of Old Testament types, prefigurements, and prophecies, from the priesthoods and tabernacle to Levitical feasts and offerings; from Messianic principles and pictures even to the complex structural architecture of the Bible itself.[108] Throughout its pages, "Christ is seen as the implicit or underlying theme of all of Scripture."[109] How could this be possible if God were not its author? Dr. Geisler documents that Christ is the theme of both testaments of the Bible as well as each of the eight major sections of Scripture. Further, Christocentric themes are found in *each* of the 66 books of the Bible!

## 12

# WHAT ARE THE SURPRISING STATISTICS ON BIBLICAL PROPHECY?

Perhaps the most definitive text on biblical prophecy is Dr. J. Barton Payne's *Encyclopedia of Biblical Prophecy*. It carefully excludes Scriptures which "do not appear to constitute valid forecasts of the future,"[110] and proceeds to cite every verse of prophecy in the Bible. It identifies 8352 predictive verses in the Bible, including 1817 total predictions and 737 separate matters predicted. Thus, "out of the OT's 23,210 verses, 6641 contain predictive material, or 28½ percent. Out of the NT's 7914 verses, 1711 contain predictive material, or 21½ percent. So for the entire Bible's 31,124 verses, 8352 contain predictive material, or 27 percent of the whole."[111]

## The Statistics of Scripture

Consider the number of prophecies in some of the following biblical books[112]:

| | Number of Predictions | Number of Predictive Verses | Total Verses | Percentage of Predictive Verses |
|---|---|---|---|---|
| Genesis | 77 | 212 | 1533 | 14 |
| Exodus | 69 | 487 | 1213 | 40 |
| Numbers | 50 | 458 | 1288 | 36 |
| Deuteronomy | 58 | 344 | 959 | 36 |
| 2 Kings | 50 | 144 | 719 | 20 |
| Psalms | 59 | 242 | 2526 | 10 |
| Isaiah | 111 | 754 | 1292 | 59 |
| Jeremiah | 90 | 812 | 1364 | 60 |
| Ezekiel | 66 | 821 | 1273 | 65 |
| Daniel | 58 | 161 | 357 | 45 |
| Hosea | 28 | 111 | 197 | 56 |
| Joel | 25 | 50 | 73 | 68 |
| Amos | 26 | 85 | 146 | 58 |

| | Number of Predictions | Number of Predictive Verses | Total Verses | Percentage of Predictive Verses |
|---|---|---|---|---|
| Obadiah | 10 | 17 | 21 | 81 |
| Micah | 40 | 73 | 105 | 70 |
| Zechariah | 78 | 144 | 211 | 69 |
| Zephaniah | 20 | 47 | 53 | 89 |
| Matthew | 81 | 278 | 1067 | 26 |
| Mark | 50 | 125 | 661 | 19 |
| Luke | 75 | 250 | 1146 | 22 |
| Acts | 63 | 125 | 1003 | 13 |
| Romans | 29 | 91 | 433 | 21 |
| Hebrews | 52 | 137 | 303 | 45 |
| Revelation | 56 | 256 | 404 | 63 |

Payne's text contains 14 tables, four statistical appendices, five complete indices, and a discussion of all 8352 predictive verses in the Bible. In the Old Testament, Ezekiel (821), Jeremiah (812), and Isaiah (754) alone contain 2,387 verses of predictive material; Zephaniah is 89 percent predictive, Obadiah 81 percent, Nahum 74 percent, and Zechariah is 69 percent predictive. In all, Isaiah contains 111 separate predictions, Jeremiah 90, Zechariah 78, and Genesis 77.[113] In the New Testament, we find that Matthew (278), Revelation (256) and Luke (250) alone contain almost 800 verses of predictive material. Payne cites more than 125 separate specific prophecies in the Old Testament about Christ's first coming, in effect proving they were prophetic and showing their fulfillment in Christ and no other person.[114] Interestingly, over 1800 verses in 29 books (including 318 verses in the New Testament) deal with the second coming of Christ. If this means anything, it means that the physical return of Jesus Christ to the earth has the same chance of being fulfilled as all the prophecies of His first coming—as we will see, a 100 percent probability.

Even the first book of the Bible contains startling predictions, yet it was written 3500 years ago—that's about the time the wheel was first invented in Samaria.

Genesis 49, for example, miraculously forecasts certain aspects of the settlement in Canaan made by the twelve tribes that were to descend from Jacob's sons. Moses, moreover, comes prior to Israel's entrance into Canaan and could therefore have had no natural knowledge of the modes of settlement...Predictions begin to appear in Genesis from its very start: eight occur in the first three chapters, even before mankind's expulsion from Eden... Predictions are involved in 212 out of the book's 1533 verses, which amounts to some 14 percent of the whole. Yet these embrace 77 distinct prophecies, more than for any other narrative portion of the OT. It exceeds the sum even for most of the overtly prophetic books of the Bible, e.g., the 66 of Ezekiel or the 56 of Revelation; and it is surpassed in count only by the major prophecies of Isaiah and Jeremiah, the detailed apocalyptic of Zechariah, and, in the NT, by the total of 81 prophecies that appear in the Gospel of Matthew.[115]

The Bible also contains numerous geopolitical prophecies. For example, Isaiah, Jeremiah, Ezekiel, Daniel, and others all predicted "future events in vivid detail, including the rise and fall of every major world empire which left its mark on the Middle East."[116] Nothing unusual here, either. Perhaps only those who have studied the tenuous and mercurial nature of geopolitical power and its historical vagaries can fully appreciate the miraculous nature of these prophecies. The prophet Daniel foresaw the rise of the Medo-Persian, Greek, and Roman empires hundreds of years before events unfolded that led to the establishment of those empires.

Dr. Payne makes the following comment upon the book of Daniel: "The last and shortest of the four Major Prophets is Daniel. It is also the one that contains the smallest percentage of predictive material: Its 58 separate forecasts involve but 162 out of the book's 357 verses, or a modest 45 percent. Chapter 7, together with its parallel in chapter 2, constitutes Scripture's most sweeping panorama of what was then future world history; and

Daniel's predictions form one of the Bible's outstanding blocks of apocalyptic literature—along with Zechariah and Revelation."[117]

For critics to maintain the Bible does not accurately predict the future is nonsense. The words are there for everyone to see. Sound critical scholarship has proven beyond a doubt when these prophecies were written, so no one can convincingly argue they were made after the fact. Only God can successfully predict the future, and He has done so in the Bible.

Of course, ancient and modern astrologers, psychics, and other prognosticators (Nostradamus, Jeane Dixon, Edgar Cayce, etc.) have also claimed they can accurately predict the future, but when pressed, they fail miserably.[118] On the other hand, the Bible is consistently accurate in its prediction of future events. Proof of this is detailed throughout many scholarly commentaries on individual biblical books and in various scholarly and popular compilations.[119]

---

## 13

---

## IS THERE EVIDENCE FOR THE DIVINE INSPIRATION OF THE BIBLE FROM FULFILLED MESSIANIC PROPHECIES?

*If one man alone had made a book of predictions about Jesus Christ, as to the time and the manner, and Jesus Christ had come in conformity to these prophecies, this fact would have infinite weight. But there is much more here. Here is a succession of men during four thousand years, who, consequently and without variation, come, one after another, to foretell this same event.*

**Blaise Pascal**

Considered by itself, Messianic prophecy alone is proof that the Bible is the Word of God and no other. How else could the 39 separate books in the Old Testament, written by more than 30 different authors beginning in 3500 B.C., all describe in detail the life and death of One Person, narrated in four separate biographies hundreds of years in the future?[120] As we indicated elsewhere, many Old Testament typologies and foreshadowings of Christ are impossible to explain unless God Himself is their author. As Dr. Arthur Pink explains:

> Of the many typical persons in the Old Testament who prefigure the Lord Jesus Christ, the striking, the accurate, and the manifold lights, in which each exhibits Him is truly remarkable...That an authentic history should supply a series of personages in different ages, whose characters, offices, and histories, should exactly correspond with those of Another who did not appear upon earth until centuries later, can only be accounted for on the supposition of Divine appointment. When we consider the utter dissimilarity of these typical persons to one another; when we note they had little or nothing in common with each other; when we remember that each of them represents some peculiar feature in a composite Antitype; we discover that we have a literary phenomenon which is truly remarkable. Abel, Isaac, Joseph, Moses, Samson, David, Solomon (and all the others) are each deficient when viewed separately; but when looked at in conjunction they form an harmonious whole, and give us a complete representation of our Lord's miraculous birth, His peerless character, His life's mission, His sacrificial death, His triumphant resurrection, His ascension to heaven, and His millennial reign. Who could have invented such characters? How remarkable that the earliest history in the world, extending from the creation and reaching to the last of the prophets—written by various hands [through] a period of fifteen centuries— should from start to finish concentrate in a single point, and that point the person and work of the blessed Redeemer! Verily, such a Book must have been written by God—no other conclusion is possible. Beneath the historical we discern the spiritual: behind the incidental we behold the typical: underneath the human biographies we see the form of Christ, and in these things we discover on every page of the Old Testament the "watermark" of heaven.[121]

Anyone can make predictions. Having them fulfilled is another story. The more statements you make about the future and the greater the detail, the better the chances proportionately, even exponentially, that you will be proven wrong. For example, think how difficult it would be for someone to predict the exact city in which the birth of a future U.S. president would take place 700 years from now. But that's what the prophet Micah did with the birthplace of the Messiah 700 years before He was born (Micah 5:2).

How difficult would it be to indicate the precise kind of death that a new, unknown religious leader would experience a thousand years from today? Could someone create and predict a new method of execution not currently known, one that wouldn't even be invented for hundreds of years? That's what King David did in 1000 B.C. when he wrote Psalm 22. Or, how difficult would it be to predict the specific date of the appearance of some great future leader hundreds of years in advance? But that's what the prophet Daniel did 530 years before Christ (Daniel 9:24-27).[122] On the other hand, if 50 specific prophecies were created about some man in the future we would never meet, how difficult would it be for that man to fulfill all 50 predictions? How hard would it be if 25 predictions were about what other people would do to him and were completely beyond his control?

For example, how could someone "arrange" to be born in a specific family (Genesis 12:2-3; 17:1, 5-7; 22:18; Matthew 1; Galatians 3:15-16)? How does someone "arrange" in advance to have his parents give birth to him in a specified city, which is not their own (Micah 5:2; Matthew 2:5-6; Luke 2:1-7)? How does one "arrange" to be virgin born (Isaiah 7:14; Matthew 1:18-24; Luke 1:26-35)? How does one plan to be considered a prophet "like Moses" (Deuteronomy 18:15 with John 1:45; 5:46; 6:14; 7:40; Acts 3:17-26; 7:37)? How does someone orchestrate (a) his own death, including being put to death by the strange method of crucifixion, (b) being put to death, not alone, but with company, specifically two criminals, and then (c) arrange to have his executioners gamble for his clothes during the execution (Psalm 22; Isaiah 53; Matthew 27:31-38; Mark 15:24)? How does one arrange to be betrayed for a specific amount of money—30 pieces of silver (Zechariah 11:13; Matthew 27:3-10)? How does one plan in advance that his executioners will carry out their regular practice of breaking the legs of the two victims on either side of him, but not his own (Psalm 34:20; John 19:33)? Finally, how does a pretender to being the Messiah arrange to be God (Isaiah 9:6; Zechariah 12:10 with John 1:1; 10:30; 14:6), and how could he possibly escape from a grave and appear to people after he has been killed (Psalm 22; Isaiah 53:9, 11; Luke 24; 1 Corinthians 15:3-8)?

It might be possible to fake one or two of these predictions, but it would be impossible for any man to arrange and fulfill all these predictions (and many others) in advance. If it can be proved that such prophecies were given of the Messiah hundreds of years in advance, and one man fulfilled all of them, then that man would logically have to be the predicted Messiah of the Old Testament.

Consider just a sampling of Jesus' fulfillment of Messianic prophecies

1. He would be born of a virgin (Isaiah 7:14; Matthew 1:23).

2. He would live in Nazareth of Galilee (Isaiah 9:1-2; Matthew 2:23; 4:15).

3. He would occasion the massacre of Bethlehem's children (Jeremiah 31:15; Matthew 2:18).

4. He would be anointed by the Holy Spirit (Isaiah 11:2; Matthew 3:16-17).

5. He would be heralded by the Lord's special messenger, John the Baptist (Isaiah 40:3; Malachi 3:1; Matthew 3:1-3).

6. His mission would include the Gentiles (Isaiah 42:1-3,6; Matthew 12:18-21). But He would be rejected by the Jews, His own people (Psalm 118:22; 1 Peter 2:7).

7. His ministry would include miracles (Isaiah 35:2-6; 61:1-2; Matthew 9:35; Luke 4:16-21).

8. He would be the Shepherd struck with the sword, resulting in the sheep being scattered (Zechariah 13:7; Matthew 26:31,56; Mark 14:27,49-50).

9. He would be betrayed by a friend for 30 pieces of silver (Zechariah 11:12-13; Matthew 27:9-10).

10. He would die a humiliating death (Psalm 22; Isaiah 53).

11. He would be rejected (Isaiah 53:3; John 1:10-11; 7:5,48).

12. He would be silent before His accusers (Isaiah 53:7; Matthew 27:12-18).

13. He would be mocked (Psalm 22:7-8; Matthew 27:31).

14. His hands and feet would be pierced (Psalm 22:16; Luke 23:33).

15. He would be crucified with thieves (Isaiah 53:12; Matthew 27:38).

16. He would pray for His persecutors (Isaiah 53:12; Luke 23:43).

17. His side would be pierced (Zechariah 12:10; John 19:34).

18. He would be buried in a rich man's tomb (Isaiah 53:9; Matthew 27:57-60).

19. Those who guarded Him would cast lots for His garments (Psalm 22:18; John 19:23-24).

20. He would be given vinegar and gall to drink (Psalm 69:21; Matthew 27:34).

21. He would rise from the dead (Psalm 16:10; Mark 16:6; Acts 2:31).

22. He would be hated without a cause (Psalm 69:4; Isaiah 49:7; John 7:48; 15:25).

23. He would be rejected by the rulers (Psalm 118:22; Matthew 21:42; John 7:48).

24. He would ascend into heaven (Psalm 68:18; Acts 1:9).

25. He would sit down at God's right hand (Psalm 110:1; Hebrews 1:3), and in the future He will be presented with dominion over all peoples, nations, and men of every language (Daniel 7:13-14; Revelation 11:15).[123]

The prophecies above are only a few of those we could list. Smith discusses 73; Payne, 191; and Edersheim, 456.[124] All these prophecies refer only to Christ's first coming. God gave a great number of prophecies about the Messiah for at least two reasons: to make identifying the Messiah obvious and to make an impostor's task impossible. This is why all other explanations than the Christian one are unproductive. Louis Lapides, former president of a national network of 15 messianic organizations, points out that even after looking at every objection critics have confronted him with, after researching the context and original languages, that "every single time, the prophecies have stood up and shown themselves to be true."[125]

---

14

---

## Is There Evidence for the Divine Inspiration of the Bible from Other Striking Prophecies?

The Bible is actually the Word of God, and the evidence cannot be explained on the basis of any other supposition. As Dr. Geisler declares in his encyclopedia of Christian evidences, "Considered as a totality, the evidences for the Bible's claim to be the Word of God are overwhelming" and "The Bible is the only book that both claims and proves to be the Word of God."[126] As noted, the existence of supernatural prophecy in the Bible cannot be denied except on the basis of an anti-supernatural bias that lacks credibility.[127] Rather than fairly examining the evidence, the critics ignore it or explain it away because they assume predictive prophecy is impossible to begin with. But they are wrong. There are many additional examples to prove them wrong and demonstrate genuine fulfilled predictions in the Bible.

## Josiah in the Book of Kings

First Kings 13:2 predicts King Josiah by name and lineage 300 years before he was even born: "...This is what the LORD says: 'A son named Josiah will be born to the house of David.'" Josiah was a contemporary of Pharaoh Neco, King of Egypt (610–595 B.C.; see 2 Kings 23:29). God also predicted that this king would destroy the altar at Bethel after sacrificing the evil prophets and burning their bones upon it. All this happened exactly as prophesied—300 years later (see 2 Kings 23:15-19).[128]

## The Babylonian Captivity in the Book of Isaiah

No one can logically deny that the internal and external evidence in the book of Isaiah clearly proves Isaiah was written approximately 700–680 B.C.[129] In other words, the book of Isaiah was indisputably in existence before the Babylonian captivity of the Jews, which began in 605 B.C. Yet in Isaiah 39:5-7, we find the Babylonian captivity itself predicted: "Then Isaiah said to Hezekiah, 'Hear the word of the LORD Almighty: The time will surely come when everything in your palace, and all that your fathers have stored up until this day, will be carried off to Babylon. Nothing will be left, says the LORD. And some of your descendants, your own flesh and blood who will be born to you, will be taken away, and they will become eunuchs in the palace of the King of Babylon'" (see Daniel 1:1-3). (Indeed, even the Assyrian conquest of Israel [722–721 B.C.] is hinted at as early as Deuteronomy 28:49-50, 64-65 [written in 1500 B.C.]: "Then the LORD will scatter you among all nations, from one end of the earth to the other. There you will worship other gods—gods of wood and stone, which neither you nor your fathers have known. Among those nations you will find no repose, no resting place for the sole of your foot.")

But Isaiah also contains specific predictions against Babylon (Isaiah 2:19-22; 14:22-23; cf. Jeremiah 51:36-44). The invincible Babylon was to be devastated by the Medes (Isaiah 13:17-22). It was to become like Sodom and Gomorrah and never to be inhabited again. Tents would not be placed there by Arabs, sheepfolds would not be present, and desert creatures would infest the ruins. Stones would not be removed for other construction projects, the ancient city would not be frequently visited, and it would be covered with swamps of water. One hundred fifty years after Isaiah's amazing prediction, the Medes and Persians besieged the walls of Babylon—considered an impossible military feat. In the exact manner predicted by Isaiah (and Jeremiah 25:11-14 and chapters 51–52), Babylon was conquered. The prophet Daniel himself recorded the specific night of the fall of Babylon: "That very night Belshazzar, king of the Babylonians, was slain, and Darius the Mede took over the kingdom, at the age of sixty-two" (Daniel 5:30-31).[130]

In *Evidence That Demands a Verdict*, Josh McDowell discusses how these and other specific predictions against Babylon were fulfilled in exact detail. The probability that these items could be fulfilled by chance alone is about one in 5 billion.[131]

### King Cyrus in Isaiah

In 700 B.C., Isaiah predicted a very important Persian king by name 120 years before he was born. The prophet predicts King Cyrus as the one who would permit the Jews to return to their land after the Babylonian captivity to rebuild Jerusalem:

> I am the LORD, who...fulfills the predictions of his messengers, who says of Jerusalem, "It shall be inhabited," of the towns of Judah, "They shall be built," and of their ruins, "I will restore them"...who says of Cyrus, "He is my shepherd and will accomplish all that I please;" he will say

of Jerusalem, "Let it be rebuilt," and of the temple, "Let its foundations be laid." (Isaiah 44:24–45:6; cf. Ezra 1:1-8).

The reason God did this is so that man will understand and know that He alone is the one true God:

> This is what the Lord says to His anointed, to Cyrus, whose right hand I take hold of to subdue nations before him.... So that you may *know* that I am the LORD, the God of Israel, who summons you *by name*. For the sake of Jacob my servant, of Israel my chosen, I summon you *by name* and bestow on you a title of honor, though you do not acknowledge me. *I am the LORD, and there is no other*, apart from me there is no God. I will strengthen you, though you have not acknowledged me, *so that* from the rising of the sun to the place of its setting *men may know* there is none besides me. I am the Lord, and there is no other (Isaiah 45:1, 3-6, emphasis added).

Jeremiah also predicted a 70-year captivity (25:11-12, 29:10-14), and Ezra records the fulfillment of this prophecy in chapter 1 of his book:

> In the first year of Cyrus king of Persia, in order to fulfill the word of the LORD spoken by Jeremiah, *the LORD moved the heart of Cyrus king of Persia to make a proclamation* throughout his realm and put it in writing: "This is what Cyrus king of Persia says: ...Let [them] go up to Jerusalem in Judah and build the temple of the LORD, the God of Israel, the God who is in Jerusalem..." (Ezra 1:1-3).

Thus, as God has predicted: "I foretold the former things long ago, my mouth announced them and I made them known; then suddenly I acted, and they came to pass" (Isaiah 48:3).

What is the probability that Isaiah could not only predict the name of a specific future king but also give wholly unexpected details concerning that king's actions toward the people of Israel 120–150 years in advance? Even skeptics will admit that such specific predicting of the future is a miracle. Perhaps skeptics might wish to reconsider their skepticism.

To determine whether a miracle such as predictive prophecy has occurred, one only need impartially investigate the evidence. For example, the founder of the Persian empire, Cyrus, reigned over the Persians from 559–530 B.C. and conquered Babylon in October of 539 B.C. Cyrus' proclamation for the Jews to return to their homeland was issued in March, 538 B.C., five months after his capture of Babylon (see Isaiah 41:2,25; 44:28–45:6,13; 46:11; Ezra 1:1-11). Thus, Isaiah predicted the return to the Holy Land 150 years before it occurred—and the one who issued the decree is named 120 years before he is even born!

## Future Kingdoms in the Book of Daniel

As a final example, consider the incredible predictions in Daniel. The internal and external evidence requires a sixth century (530) B.C. composition. Yet the prophet Daniel predicts the Medo-Persian, Greek, and Roman Empires in such detail that anti-supernaturalists are forced, against all the evidence, to date the book at 165 B.C., implying it is essentially a forgery. Anyone who studies Daniel, chapters 2, 7, 8, and 11 in light of subsequent Medo-Persian, Greek, and Roman history, including the dynasties of the Egyptians and the Syrians (the Ptolemies and Seleucids), cannot fail to be amazed. The NIV Study Bible (Grand Rapids, MI: Zondervan Publishing House, 1995) text notes, which are based on the accumulated scholarship of more than 100 authorities, observe: "The widely held view that the book of Daniel is largely fictional rests mainly on the modern philosophical assumption that long-range predictive prophecy is impossible....But objective evidence excludes this hypothesis on several counts...."[132]

Thus, no one can logically deny the Bible has accurately predicted future world military powers such as the Medo-Persians, Alexander's Greece, and the Roman Empire in Daniel 2 and 7. Indeed, "[The great Jewish historian] Josephus adds that the [Jewish] priests showed Alexander [the Great] the prophecies in

Daniel concerning a Greek conquering the Persian Empire. This pleased Alexander, and he treated the Jews with kindness."[133]

But there is a more relevant point here for us personally. If Daniel so easily predicted the military and political lineups in the succeeding centuries of his own period, then he and other biblical prophets can be expected to just as easily have predicted the military and geopolitical lineup immediately preceding the return of Christ Himself. (And it looks as if we may indeed be approaching that line-up; see Dr. Arnold Fruchtenbaum's six-year study, *The Footsteps of the Messiah: A Study of the Sequence of Prophetic Events*, and other works.)[134]

Consider the comments of Dr. Gleason Archer concerning the evidence for Daniel's predictive prophecy. Dr. Archer is a scholar who received his Ph.D. in comparative literature from Harvard University and has spent 30 years teaching on the graduate seminary level in the field of biblical criticism. He has received training in Latin, Greek, French, and German; in seminary he majored in Hebrew, Aramaic, and Arabic. In all, he reads 15 different languages.[135] Dr. Archer reveals of Daniel:

> The linguistic evidence from Qumran makes the rationalistic explanation for Daniel [that it was written 165 B.C.] no longer tenable. It is difficult to see how any scholar can defend this view and maintain intellectual respectability... The symbolism of Chapter 7 and Chapter 8 points unmistakably to the identification of the second kingdom as Medo-Persian and the third as Greek...For this amazing pattern of prediction and fulfillment, there can be no successful answer on the part of the critics who espouse the Maccabean date hypothesis [165 B.C.]. There is no evading the conclusion that the prophecies of the Book of Daniel were inspired by the same God who later fulfilled them, or who will fulfill them in the last days, which are destined to close our present era with the final great conflict of Armageddon and second coming of our Lord Jesus Christ.[136]

Of course, the same conclusion of Daniel's prophetic accuracy was reached many decades ago by the famed Princeton scholar, Dr. Robert Dick Wilson, who was fluent in many languages including all the Biblical and cognate languages—Hebrew, Aramaic, Sumerian/Babylonian dialects, Ethiopic, Phoenician, Assyrian, various Egyptian and Persian dialects, etc.—45 languages/dialects in all. He openly challenged any person living to set forth an argument that he could not personally investigate and refute that would undermine the integrity and accuracy of the prophetic text of Daniel, or indeed of any book of the Old Testament.[137] Scholars such as Wilson, K.A. Kitchen, Charles Boutflower, and others have literally demolished critical arguments against Daniel's predictions.[138] The historical, archæological, and linguistic evidences all support the conclusion that Daniel's prophecies are genuine.

---

## 15

## HOW HARD IS IT TO MAKE SUCH PREDICTIONS BY GUESSING?

How can anyone account for these startling predictions if the Bible is only written by men who were guessing, even using their best powers of deduction? Cyrus is predicted 120 years beforehand, Josiah 300 years, Bethlehem 700 years, and the Medo-Persian, Greek, and Roman empires hundreds of years before they existed. Anyone who takes the time to sit down and attempt to calculate specific future events, persons, and political alliances and kingdoms will discover the sheer impossibility of the task. To illustrate, the late Canadian scholar Dr. Arthur Custance observes that most people have never really considered the difficulty of the task faced by the biblical prophets if they were *not* subject to divine inspiration.

> Human history is not repetitive. Like culture, it is cumulative. Experience grows, not only in the individual, but in

societies and nations, so that no situation can ever be exactly repeated a second time. Consequently there is always something unpredictable, because a new element is added with every consecutive moment of unfolding. Although it may appear a simple matter to predict what will happen a few years from now in some particular context, in actual fact it becomes more and more impossible as one tries to be more and more explicit. Generalizations are easy, and their fulfillment can be claimed when events bear any semblance at all to the prediction. But the mind somehow refuses to create any exact picture of the future. It sounds simple, yet the difficulty can be verified experimentally by anybody who is willing to make the attempt to put down on a piece of paper some striking event that he is prepared to state will happen on his own street or in his own home one year from the present—excluding natural events. If the one-year limit is too restricting, try ten years. If this won't work, enlarge your horizon to include your city, not just your street; or, if you like, take the world. I believe this simple test will demonstrate to any honest mind the sheer impossibility of predicting history in any specific detail unless one falls back upon making pretty safe assumptions about events linked directly to situations of which one is able to make reasonable "extensions."

And he concludes, "Biblical prophecies are not this, and the distinction is of fundamental importance."[139]

Further, one appreciates these prophecies all the more when one realizes they were often entirely unexpected possibilities when first given. For example, Isaiah predicted the Babylonian captivity when Babylon was a somewhat obscure power and gave no indication of its future greatness. One may as well make a similar prediction that Nicaragua will soon become a world power. No one today would risk one's reputation by making such an ill-advised prediction. However, the biblical prophets did make such predictions because God told them what would happen. By the time of Jeremiah, Babylon had become a great world power, but there was no evidence that Babylon would be destroyed. To the contrary, the Babylonian empire was considered invincible. However, Jeremiah said Babylon would soon be destroyed because of the manner in which she treated Israel (Jeremiah 50–51). Ezekiel, too, confirmed this prediction and also declared, quite out of harmony with expectation, that the city of Tyre would be destroyed, giving extremely specific prophecies—all of which were exactly fulfilled (Ezekiel 26–28).[140] For example, in Ezekiel chapter 26, a number of things are stated: that Nebuchadnezzar would destroy the city of Tyre, that many nations would be against Tyre, that Tyre would be laid bare like the top of a flat rock, that fishermen would spread nets over the site, that the debris of Tyre would be thrown into the water, and that it would never be rebuilt. As Dr. Custance, McDowell, and others have pointed out by citing various historical sources, all these predictions were literally fulfilled, principally by Nebuchadnezzar first, and later by Alexander the Great.[141]

In Ezekiel chapters 25–32, the prophet makes specific prophecies against the Mediterranean nations of Ammon, Moab, Edom, Philistia, Tyre, and Egypt. As one reads the prophecies, one wonders how Ezekiel could possibly have known all this on his own, for his prophecies were literally fulfilled. Robert W. Manweiler has a Ph.D. in physics from Cornell University and is a graduate of respected Westminster Seminary. He points out that "centuries of scholarship have found no good reason to date the book later than the time of Ezekiel. Instead it has been regarded as a remarkably historical book." Further, he shows that the historical data proving the accuracy of the prophecies come from secular historical records, not from Christians or Jews:

> [The] historical records narrating events fulfilling these prophecies are detailed and well-documented, particularly with respect to the most unusual statements. These narratives are in full agreement with the prophecies, and they were not written by Christians, Jews or Muslims who might be suspected of trying to make Ezekiel look good... The Bible believer, then, is not blindly trusting anyone who

claims to have had a revelation. He or she is accepting
Scripture on the basis of strong verification that it comes
from One who knows, the God who controls history."[142]

What these predictions indicate is that because the Bible already
has demonstrated accuracy in prediction, there is no basis for
assuming that its future prophecies will not be just as accurately
fulfilled. Most of these yet-unfulfilled prophecies could actually be
fulfilled in our lifetime, so they should be taken seriously.

Obviously, we should not present supernatural explanations
where we do not have to. However, when we are forced to a supernatural explanation in order to effectively explain the facts, then
denying it only means we have no explanation for the facts. But to
prefer ignorance to explanation and enlightenment is contrary to
good judgment.

The Bible is the only sacred religious book on earth with concrete evidence of divine inspiration by supernatural prediction.
The closest competitor is the Koran. But of the alleged prophecies
in the Koran, only one is substantive (the Roman victory at Issus
in Sura 30:2-4). However, this is not convincing as supernatural
prophecy because it was expected and did not fulfill the time span
given. It wasn't an accurate prediction. Collectively, the prophecies
claimed in the Koran are either vague and disputable, have
expected results (such as victory in battle), or fail the predictions.[143]

In conclusion, comparing the prophecies in the Bible to those
in all other sacred books calls attention to one main point: the
insurmountable difficulty of prediction apart from divine inspiration.

---

16

---

## How Can the Bible Be Without Error?

If the Bible is really the Word of God, inerrancy is what one
might expect.

But what an inconceivably difficult proposition to defend in a modern, scientific world. Could 40-plus writers, from highly divergent backgrounds and temperaments—kings, tax collectors, prophets, physicians, exiles, fishermen—writing over a period of 1500 years from 1450 B.C. to 50 A.D. on scores of different subjects, in widely varying and difficult circumstances, writing history in extremely specific detail, even giving hundreds of predictions of the future—plus much more that would make errors a certainty—could all of them to the last man have written something the size of the Bible without a single error? Talk about a miracle! Try that with 66 books and 40 authors over 1500 years with any other group of writers!

There are three principal lines of evidence for the inerrancy of the Bible, properly understood:[144] 1) the Bible's own claim to be the literal word of God, given its credibility in other areas, 2) the testimony of Jesus, based on His authority, and 3) the lack of a single proven error, despite innumerable critical examinations by both skeptics and believers.

First, the Bible claims to be inerrant because it is fully inspired by a truthful God who declares He cannot lie (Numbers 23:19; Hebrews 6:18; Titus 1:2; 2 Timothy 2:13). For example:

- All Scripture is inspired by God...[145] (2 Timothy 3:16-17 NASB).

- The Scripture cannot be broken...(John 10:35).

- Every word of God is tested...(Proverbs 30:5 NASB).

- The words of the LORD are pure words, as silver tried in a furnace on the earth, refined seven times (Psalm 12:6 NASB).

- For you have been born again not of seed which is perishable but imperishable, that is, through the living and abiding word of God (1 Peter 1:23 NASB).

- Forever O LORD, Your word is settled in heaven (Psalm 119:89 NASB).

- For truly I say to you, until heaven and earth pass away, not the smallest letter or stroke shall pass away from the law until all is accomplished (Matthew 5:18 NASB).

- For I did not speak on My own initiative, but the Father Himself who sent Me has given Me a commandment as to what to say and what to speak. I know that His commandment is eternal life; therefore the things I speak, I speak just as the Father has told Me (John 12:49-50 NASB).

- Thy word is Truth (John 17:17 NASB).

- But He answered and said, "It is written, 'Man shall not live on bread alone, but on every word that proceeds out of the mouth of God'" (Matthew 4:4 NASB).

- But the Word of the Lord abides forever (1 Peter 1:25 NASB).

Second, the inerrancy of the Bible is evidenced by Jesus' own absolute trust in and use of Scripture.[146] If there were errors in Scripture, Jesus would have noted and corrected them, but even this is unthinkable for it presumes either errant divine inspiration or a lack of providential preservation of the text (cf. John 14:26). For Jesus, what Scripture said, God said—period. Not once did He say, "This Scripture is in error," and proceed to correct it. In *Christ and the Bible,* a detailed, authoritative study of this, John Wenham points out,

> Surely He would have explained clearly a mingling of divine truth and human error in Scripture had He thought such to exist. The notion that our Lord was fully aware that the view of Holy Scripture current in His day was erroneous, and that He deliberately accommodated His teaching to the beliefs of his hearers, will not square with

the facts. His use of the Old Testament seems altogether too insistent, positive, and absolute.[147]

It is of the Old Testament without any reservation or exception that he says, it "cannot be broken"...He affirms the unbreakableness of the Scripture in its entirety and leaves no room for any such supposition as that of degrees of inspiration and fallibility. Scripture is inviolable. Nothing less than this is the testimony of our Lord. And the crucial nature of such witness is driven home by the fact that it is in answer to the most serious of charges and in the defense of his most stupendous claim that he bears this testimony.[148]

Dr. John Warwick Montgomery makes the highly relevant observation that because of His divine authority, "the weight of Christ's testimony to Scripture is so much more powerful than any alleged contradiction or error in the text or any combination of them, that the latter must be adjusted to the former, not the reverse."[149] Here is why.

The evidence for inerrancy is that no error has ever been proven in the Bible. This is another state of affairs that can virtually be considered a miracle. As far as we know, no ancient text of some length and detail is without error. Indeed, it is simply impossible to account for books like Zephaniah, Obadiah, and Nahum that are over 70 percent predictive apart from an omniscient God who knows the future. All it takes is one undeniably false prophecy, and inerrancy is undermined. But many scholars have critically investigated the biblical text and still declared that the Bible is inerrant.

Gleason L. Archer was an undergraduate classics major who received training in Latin, Greek, French, and German at Harvard University. At seminary he majored in Hebrew, Aramaic, and Arabic, and in post-graduate study became involved with Akkadian and Syriac, teaching courses on these subjects. He has had a special interest in middle kingdom Egyptian studies and at the Oriental Institute in Chicago did specialized study in Eighteenth

Dynasty historical records, as well as studying Coptic and Sumerian. He has also visited the Holy Land, where he toured most of the important archaeological sites, and spent time in Beirut, Lebanon, for a specialized study of modern literary Arabic. He holds a degree from Princeton Theological Seminary and a Ph.D. from Harvard Graduate School. This background enabled him to become expert in the issue of alleged errors or contradictions in Scripture.

Regarding alleged errors in the extant copies of Scripture he says,

> In my opinion this charge can be refuted and its falsity exposed by an objective study done in a consistent, evangelical perspective...I candidly believe I have been confronted with just about all the biblical difficulties under discussion in theological circles today—especially those pertaining to the interpretation and defense of Scripture...As I have dealt with one apparent discrepancy after another and have studied the alleged contradictions between the biblical record and the evidence of linguistics, archæology, or science, my confidence in the trustworthiness of Scripture has been repeatedly verified and strengthened by the discovery that almost every problem in Scripture that has ever been discovered by man, from ancient times until now, has been dealt with in a completely satisfactory manner by the biblical text itself—or else by objective archæological information.[150]

Dr. Robert Dick Wilson, an Old Testament authority and author of *A Scientific Investigation of the Old Testament*, could read the New Testament in nine different languages by the age of 25. In addition, he could repeat from memory a Hebrew translation of the entire New Testament without missing a single syllable and do the same with large portions of the Old Testament. He proceeded to learn 45 languages and dialects and was also a master of paleography and philology.

> For 45 years continuously, since I left college, I have devoted myself to the one great study of the Old Testament, in all its languages, in all its archaeology, in all its translations, and as far as possible in everything bearing upon its text and history…I have made it an invariable habit never to accept an objection to a statement of the Old Testament without subjecting it to a most thorough investigation, linguistically and factually…I defy any man to make an attack upon the Old Testament on the grounds of evidence that I cannot investigate.

His conclusion was that no critic has succeeded in proving an error in the Old Testament.[151]

Theologian, philosopher, and trial attorney John Warwick Montgomery, holding nine graduate degrees in different fields, observes, "I myself have never encountered an alleged contradiction in the Bible which could not be cleared up by the use of the original languages of the Scriptures and/or by the use of accepted principals of literary and historical interpretation."[152]

Benjamin B. Warfield, the great Princeton University theologian who held five doctorate degrees, resolutely affirmed inerrancy[153] and authored the classic text, *The Inspiration and Authority of the Bible*.

Rev. John W. Haley examined 900 alleged problems in Scripture, concluding, "I cannot but avow, as the [conclusion] of my investigation, the profound conviction that every difficulty and discrepancy in the Scriptures is…capable of a fair and reasonable solution."[154] Noted Greek scholar Dr. William Arndt of *A Greek-English Lexicon of the New Testament and Other Early Christian Literature* fame, concluded in his own study of alleged contradictions and errors in the Bible, "[W]e may say with full conviction that no instances of this sort occur anywhere in the Scriptures."[155]

Dr. Harold O. J. Brown earned four degrees from Harvard University and Harvard Divinity School and studied at the University of Marburg, Germany, and the University of Vienna, Austria. He concluded, "If it were possible to point to undeniable, substantial errors in the present Hebrew and Greek texts of Scripture, it would certainly suggest the presumption that the originals had errors. The fact that it is still possible today to claim the autographs were inerrant is an indication that no one has yet succeeded in showing there is even one substantial, undeniable error or contradiction in our present copies."[156]

Noted theologian J. I. Packer concluded, "No compelling necessity springs from modern knowledge to conclude that Scripture errs anywhere..."[157]

In conclusion, a trinity of factors—1) the miraculous nature of the Bible itself, which speaks for its inspiration and hence inerrancy, 2) the infallible pronouncements of God incarnate on an inerrant Scripture, and 3) the minute examination of the data of the text itself, are sufficient reasons to accept the proposition that the Bible is inerrant.

---

### 17

## IS THE UNIQUENESS OF THE BIBLE UNRIVALED?

The following 20 points, briefly summarized, reveal just how unique the Bible is.

1. The Bible is the only book in the world that offers objective evidence to be the Word of God. Only the Bible gives real proof of its divine inspiration.

2. The Bible is the only Scripture in the world that is inerrant.

3. The Bible is the only book that can claim that its teachings are prefigured in other cultures, religions, and even archtypes.[158]

4. The Bible is the only Scripture that offers eternal salvation as a gift given entirely by God's grace and mercy.

5. The Bible is the only major ancient religious Scripture whose complete textual preservation is established as virtually autographic.

6. The Bible contains the greatest moral standards of any book.

7. Only the Bible begins with the creation of the universe by divine fiat and contains a continuous, if often brief and interspersed, historical record of mankind from the first man, Adam, to the end of history.

8. Only the Bible contains detailed prophecies about the coming Savior of the world, whose prophecies have proven true in history.

9. The Bible has the most realistic view of human nature, the power to convict people of their sin, and the ability to change human nature. Only the Bible offers a realistic and permanent solution to the problem of human sin and evil.

10. The Bible has a unique theological content including its theology proper (the Trinity and God's attributes), soteriology (depravity, imputation, grace, propitiation/atonement, reconciliation, regeneration, union with Christ, justification, adoption, sanctification, eternal security, election, etc.), Christology (the incarnation and hypostatic union), pneumatology (the Person and Work of the Holy Spirit), eschatology (detailed predictions of the end of history), and ecclesiology (the nature of the Church as Christ's bride and its organic union with Him).

11. Only the Bible has its accuracy confirmed in history by archæology, textual criticism, science, and the like.

12. The Bible is unique in its unity and internal consistency despite its production over a 1500-year period by 40-plus

authors in three languages on three continents discussing scores of controversial subjects.

13. The Bible is the most translated, purchased, memorized,
and persecuted book in history. For example, it is translated into some 1700 languages, leaving all other ancient
or modern books or scriptures in the dust.

14. Only the Bible is fully one-quarter prophetic, that is,
containing a total of some 400 *pages* of predictive material.

15. Only the Bible has withstood 2000 years of intense scrutiny by critics and not only survived the attacks but pros-
pered and had its credibility strengthened by such
criticism. (Voltaire predicted the Bible would be extinct
within 100 years; within 50 years Voltaire was extinct and
his house was a warehouse for the Bibles of the Geneva
Bible Society.)

16. The Bible has had more influence in the world than any
other book; it has molded the history of Western civilization.

17. Only the Bible has a person-specific (Christ-centered)
nature for each of its 66 books detailing the person's life
in prophecy, type, anti-type, and so on, 400–1500 years
before the person was born.

18. Only the Bible proclaims a historically proven resurrection of its central figure.

19. Only the Bible provides historic proof that the one true
God loves mankind.

20. The Bible is the only ancient book with documented scientific and medical prevision. No other ancient book is
ever carefully analyzed along scientific lines, but many

books have been written on the theme of the Bible and modern science.

## 18

## CAN THE BIBLE'S TEACHINGS ON SCIENCE PROVE IT IS DIVINELY INSPIRED?

The Bible is obviously not a science text, and further it "only affirms partial truth in the areas of science."[159] Still, no fact of science proves it is wrong. This is miraculous, given the amount of scientific prevision found in its pages. As Dr. Geisler points out, "Given that not much scientific information was known in Bible times, the Bible speaks with considerable scientific credibility, an evidence of its supernatural nature."[160]

Scientists themselves have frequently been impressed by the scientific accuracy of the Bible. One example is A.E. Wilder-Smith, who earned three doctorates in science and wrote *The Reliability of the Bible*. Hugh Ross, Ph.D., was at 17 the youngest person ever to serve as director of observations for Vancouver's Royal Astronomical Society. At Caltech he researched quasars for postdoctoral studies and was later a Research Fellow in Radio Astronomy at the California Institute of Technology. He recalls that when he first investigated the Bible as an unbeliever while he was "testing" various sacred books for scientific and historical accuracy,

> I found the Bible noticeably different. It was simple, direct, and specific. I was amazed at the quantity of historical and scientific (testable) material it included and at the detail of this material...For the next year and a half I spent about an hour a day searching the Bible for scientific and historical inaccuracies. I finally had to admit that it was error free and that this perfect accuracy could only come from the Creator Himself...Further, I had proven to myself, on

the basis of predicted history and science, that the Bible was more reliable than many of the laws of physics. My only rational option was to trust the Bible's authority to the same degree as I trusted the laws of physics.[161]

Another example is Kurt Wise, Ph.D., Director of Origins Research and Associate Professor of Science, Division of Mathematics and Natural Science, Bryan College, Dayton, Tennessee. Another is noted scientist and creationist, Dr. Henry Morris, author of some 50 books on science and the Bible, including *The Bible and Modern Science, Men of Science, Men of God: Great Scientists Who Believed the Bible, The Biblical Basis for Modern Science,* and *Many Infallible Proofs: Evidences for the Christian Faith.*

Citations could be multiplied into the thousands, so let us go to the evidence.

Chuck Missler worked as Branch Chief of the Air Force Department of Guided Missiles, as a systems engineer with TRW, a large aerospace firm, as a senior analyst for the Department of Defense, and established the first international computer network in 1966. In *The Creator Beyond Time and Space,* he and Mark Eastman, M.D. provide a number of examples illustrating how, scientifically speaking, the Bible was thousands of years ahead of its time. They note

There are dozens of passages in the Bible which demonstrate tremendous scientific foreknowledge…We find that the scientific statements in the Bible are without error or contradiction…When the biblical text is carefully examined the reader will quickly discover an uncanny scientific accuracy unparalleled by any document of antiquity…the Bible does describe scientific phenomena in common terminology with unmistakable clarity…In virtually all ancient religious documents it is common to find scientifically inaccurate myths about the nature of the universe and the life forms on planet earth. Any cursory review of ancient mythology will readily confirm this statement. However, the Bible is unique because of the conspicuous absence of such myths. In fact, throughout the Bible we find scientifically accurate concepts about the physical universe that were not "discovered" by modern scientists until very recent times.[162]

Consider some examples:[163]

As to Psalm 102:25-26, Isaiah 51:6, and Matthew 24:35, which declare heaven and earth will pass away, Eastman and Missler comment,

> It is fascinating to find such accurate scientific descriptions of the universe. Prior to the twentieth century, the notion that the universe is "wearing out" or "passing away" was foreign to the minds of most scientists and philosophers. Such scientific foreknowledge could not have been derived from observation or intuition. When the Bible was being penned there was no observable evidence that the universe was wearing out. In fact, the consensus of the world's scientists and philosophers was that it was not decaying.[164]

Jeremiah 33:22 says that "the host of heaven cannot be numbered" (KJV). Jeremiah wrote in the eighth century B.C. when astronomers believed that it was possible to number the stars. Today we know there are at least 100 billion stars in our galaxy and probably several hundred billion galaxies in the universe. For anyone to number the stars would probably take trillions of years.

Some 3000 years ago, the Psalmist wrote that the sun follows a circular path through the universe. "It rises at one end of the heavens and makes its circuit to the other; nothing is hidden from its heat" (Psalm 19:6). Today we know that the sun does move in a "circuit" at speeds close to 600,000 miles per hour within one of the spiral arms of the Milky Way galaxy. That galaxy itself is hurling through space at over a million miles per hour. (It has always amazed me [Weldon] that I can safely visit the beach each day, and stand right there on the edge of trillions of tons of water, and watch a feather drop. I can hardly walk a full bowl of soup a few yards without spilling it. But the oceanic "soup bowl" has variant, inconceivable centrifugal forces on it, yet it stays in place. Jets fly off aircraft carriers accelerating from zero to 150 miles per hour in two seconds—that's fast. But the earth is spinning about 1000 miles per hour, orbiting the sun in another direction at about 67,000 miles per hour [30 times faster than a rifle bullet— most people don't realize it, but just traveling around the sun, we each journey about 40 *billion* miles during our lifetime], cruises another route at about 560,000 miles per hour (our solar system's course within the Milky Way galaxy), speeds another direction at about 665,000 miles per hour (the Milky Way galaxy moving within the local galaxy group), and that local cluster of galaxies is moving at greater speeds to a larger cluster in the constellation Virgo. Yet despite all these speeds and forces, trillions of tons of water remain within the boundaries of a few yards from my feet. [Try making a small scale replica of the earth, a sphere with 70 percent water, and throwing it a few feet.] We can explain it, thanks to gravity and other factors. But although the miracle stands "explained," it seems nonetheless miraculous. Truth be told, there are tens of thousands of such miracles, from mind-boggling information concerning how living things function on land and in the oceans, to utterly astonishing facts of the earth and outer space, to beyond belief conundrums of the "immaterial" worlds in sub-atomic physics. Indeed, had the World Trade Center's twin towers been built of spider's web, they would not have been penetrated by the hijacked aircraft.[165] Even the lowly spider's web is 100 times stronger than steel by weight. All by chance? I don't think so.)

At the time Job and Isaiah wrote, it was commonly believed that the earth rested upon something, whether an elephant, a turtle, or the muscular back of Atlas. The earth was also flat. Yet in Isaiah 40:22, written in 700 B.C., we read, "He sits enthroned above the circle of the earth, and its people are like grasshoppers. He stretches out the heavens like a canopy, and spreads them out like a tent to live in." The Hebrew *khug*, often translated circle, literally means sphere. In Job 26:7 we also read, "He spreads out the northern skies over empty space; he suspends the earth over nothing." In 700 B.C., the biblical view must have been somewhat startling to read. Isaiah wrote 28 centuries ago and Job is probably the oldest book in the Bible. How could the biblical writers have made educated guesses about this? Indeed, in *The Remarkable Record of Job*, scientist Dr. Henry Morris points out that in Job alone there are some two dozen disclosures of scientific fore-knowledge.

In Hebrews 11:3 we read, "By faith we understand that the universe was formed at God's command, so that what is seen was not made out of what was visible." The author is correct when he describes the fact that what we can see—matter—is made of particles that aren't visible in natural light.

In 2 Peter 3:10 we find, "But the day of the Lord will come like a thief. The heavens will disappear with a roar; the elements will be destroyed by fire, and the earth and everything in it will be laid bare." Written 2000 years ago, when the beliefs concerning the nature of matter were rather crude, it is amazing to find descriptions such as these. The Apostle Peter seems to be describing what happens when the nucleus of radioactive elements are split, discharging staggering amounts of energy and radioactivity.

In Psalm 8:8 we read of "the birds of the air, and the fish of the sea, all that swim the paths of the seas." Not until the mid-nineteenth century did Matthew Fontaine Maury, the "father of oceanography," publish his discovery that the ocean has predictable paths or currents. When Psalm 8 was written, the only seas known to the Hebrews were the Dead Sea, the Sea of Galilee, the Mediterranean, and the Red Sea. They did not possess "paths" or significant observable currents.

In Job 36:27-28 we read, "He draws up the drops of water, which distill as rain to the streams; the clouds pour down their moisture and abundant showers fall on mankind." Here we find a correct depiction of the earth's hydrologic cycle. In the Middle Ages the source of rainwater was something of a mystery, but almost 3500 years earlier Job describes the rain cycle.

In Ecclesiastes 1:6-7, "The wind blows to the south and turns to the north; round and round it goes, ever returning on its course. All streams flow into the sea, yet the sea is never full. To the place the streams come from, there they return again." King Solomon, writing 3000 years ago, speaks of global wind currents and the earth's water cycle. "The phrase, 'the wind blows to the south and turns to the north; round and round it goes, ever returning on its course' is an accurate and astonishing description of the circular flow of air around the earth, called the 'jet stream,' well known to anyone who watches the evening news weather reports."[166]

So far we have briefly looked at aspects of cosmology, physics, oceanography, and the hydrologic cycle. We find similar scientific prevision in other sciences. Consider this example from the world of medicine. God had directed Abraham to circumcise newborn males specifically on the eighth day (Genesis 17:12). It wasn't until the twentieth century that we discovered that only after eight days of life does vitamin K in the infant's diet permit prothrombin, an important blood-clotting factor, to reach its peak. To circumcise on an earlier day, when the clotting mechanism is immature, could result in excessive bleeding. Further, there are many other cultures that circumcise their males on the first, fourth, sixth, seventh, or twentieth days of life. If the Jews had discovered the eighth day merely by trial and error, why didn't other cultures do so? Clearly, Jewish practice was based on obedience to divine revelation. Deuteronomy 23:12-14, Leviticus 17:11, and many other Scriptures reflect hygienic or medical knowledge far in advance of their time.

In his 500-page text, *The Biblical Basis for Modern Science*, Dr. Henry Morris supplies a large number of additional examples of scientific foreknowledge or allusions in the Bible. A sampling is given in his *Many Infallible Proofs*.[167]

Certainly, for skeptics to successfully argue that the Bible is *not* the inspired Word of God, they must explain how the Bible contains statements such as these, which were often disharmonious with the accepted knowledge of the time in which they were written—and yet so accurate in light of today's facts of science. In essence,

> To argue that the evidences for biblical inspiration are the result of a myriad of lucky guesses requires an enormous measure of faith. Such an assertion requires us to believe that ancient fishermen, tent makers, shepherds, kings and paupers, who were separated by 1500 years on three different continents, could consistently, and without error, describe the nature of the universe, planet Earth and its life forms, in a way that is fully consistent with twentieth-century science. It requires us to believe that those same men wrote history in advance—all of this without the guidance of One with supernatural "inside information."[168]

---

## 19

## WERE THE BRANCHES OF SCIENCE USUALLY FOUNDED BY CHRISTIANS WHO BELIEVED THE BIBLE WAS THE LITERAL WORD OF GOD?

In light of the Bible's scientific prevision, it is relevant to note that many of the branches of modern science were founded by Bible-believing Christians, as documented in Dr. Morris' *Men of Science, Men of God: Great Scientists Who Believed the Bible* (from which most of the listing below is taken) and other books. Several actually founded a scientific discipline specifically because of biblical statements, such as Maury, Maxwell, and Simpson. Daniel Graves wrote *Scientists of Faith: Forty-Eight Biographies of Historic Scientists and Their Christian Faith.* In "Christian Influences in the Sciences" at the rae.org website he supplies about 150 examples of critical Christian influence in the sciences. "There is hardly a science or scientific idea which cannot trace its inception as a viable theory to some Christian."[169] Graves also wrote *Doctors Who Followed Christ: Thirty-Two Biographies of Eminent Physicians and Their Christian Faith* which includes Surgeon General C. Everett

Koop and the conquerors of various diseases, including Edward Jenner (smallpox) and Walter Reed (yellow fever). The five greatest physicists in history—Newton, Faraday, Thompson, Maxwell, and Einstein—were each candid in their belief that the universe was created by God; four of the five were committed Christians with a firm conviction that the Bible was the authoritative Word of God. Below, we cite 25 examples. Collectively these scientists, like many scientists today, upheld the biblical view of creation, were involved in supporting Christian missionary work, wrote books on Christian evidences, believed in Jesus Christ as their personal Savior from sin, and had their own personal ministries in church.

1. Johannes Kepler (1571–1630), founder of physical astronomy

2. Robert Boyle (1627–1691), father of modern chemistry

3. Blaise Pascal (1623–1662), an early great mathematician who laid the foundations for things like hydrodynamics, differential calculus, and probability theory

4. John Ray (1627–1705), father of English natural history and probably the best zoologist and botanist of his time

5. Nicolaus Steno (1631–1686), father of stratigraphy

6. William Petty (1623–1687) helped institute the science of statistics and the modern study of economics

7. Isaac Newton (1642–1727) invented calculus, discovered the law of gravity and the three laws of motion, developed the particle theory of light propagation, invented the reflecting telescope, etc.

8. Carolus Linnaeus (1707–1778), father of biological taxonomy

9. Michael Faraday (1791–1867), one of the greatest physicists, developed essential concepts in electricity and

magnetism, invented the electrical generator, and made numerous contributions to chemistry

10. Georges Cuvier (1769–1832), founder of comparative anatomy

11. Charles Babbage (1792–1871), founder of computer science

12. John Dalton (1766–1844), father of atomic theory

13. Matthew Maury (1806–1873), founder of oceanography

14. James Simpson (1811–1879) discovered chloroform, laying the groundwork for anesthesiology

15. James Joule (1818–1889) discovered the mechanical equivalent of heat, laying the foundation for the field of thermodynamics

16. Louis Agassiz (1807–1873), father of glacial geology

17. Gregor Mendel (1822–1884), father of genetics

18. Louis Pasteur (1822–1895), father of bacteriology

19. Joseph Lister (1827–1912) founder of antiseptic surgical methods (Pasteur's and Lister's contributions, incidentally, have saved millions of lives.)

20. William Thompson, Lord Kelvin (1824–1907), one of the greatest physicists who established thermodynamics on a formal scientific basis, supplying a strict statement of the first two laws of thermodynamics

21. Joseph Clerk Maxwell (1831–1879) created a systematic theoretical and mathematical organization for electromagnetic field theory. Einstein praised Maxwell's contributions as the best in physics since Newton.

22. Bernhard Riemann (1826–1866) developer of non-Euclidian geometry, used by Einstein in his development of relativity theory

23. Joseph Henry Gilbert (1817–1901) developed nitrogen and superphosphate fertilizers for farm crops; codeveloped the first agricultural experimental station, laying a foundation for the advances in agricultural science that allowed farmers to feed millions

24. John Ambrose Fleming (1849–1945) invented the Fleming valve laying the foundation for ensuing developments in electronics

25. Wernher Von Braun (1912–1977), father of space science

# THE PERSON OF JESUS CHRIST

---

## 20

---

## HOW INFLUENTIAL IS JESUS CHRIST AND WHAT SURPRISING THINGS DID HE CLAIM?

*The contemplation of things as they are, without substitution or imposture, without error or confusion, is in itself a nobler thing than a whole harvest of invention.*

**Francis Bacon**

Jesus is the single most commanding person in the whole history of mankind. It is not too much to say that if Jesus Christ had never been born, our entire Western civilization would not exist as it does—nor would many of the advancements in the rest of the world. As Dr. D. James Kennedy points out in *What If Jesus Had Never Been Born?*

> Jesus Christ, the greatest man who ever lived, has changed virtually every aspect of human life—and most people don't know it...Nineteen centuries have come and gone, and today He is the central figure of the human race. All the armies that ever marched, all the navies that ever sailed, all the parliaments that ever sat, all the kings that ever reigned, put together, have not affected the life of man on this earth as much as that one solitary life.[170]

The influence of Christ and Christianity in helping the poor, the founding of America, the expansion of civil liberties, education and science, health and medicine, economics, the family and morality, the arts and other areas is far greater than the average person suspects. When the three major news magazines—*Time, Newsweek,* and *U.S. News & World Report*—carried cover stories on the same person (Jesus Christ) for the same issue (April 8, 1996), it may have been unique in the history of secular publishing, and it could never have happened with any other individual born 2000 years ago. If Jesus was only who the secularists and religious liberals claim He was, it could never have happened at all.

But, as we will see, Jesus Christ makes stupendous claims about Himself. These compel us to conclude that our relationship to Christ, or lack of it, will dramatically affect our present and future existence. His life is far more vital to our life, as well as the lives of our friends and family, than we may realize. Jesus Christ is that important, and the evidence concurs.

As we saw, evaluating the claims of Jesus, readers should understand that even skeptics can't rationally deny that the four Gospel biographies of Christ are based on accurate historical reporting. At least two, Matthew and John, were written by those who knew Christ closely and personally and had traveled with Him daily for more than three years. In completing his biography, the Apostle Luke asserts that he "carefully investigated everything from the beginning" (Luke 1:3), and it is generally agreed that the Apostle Mark got the information for his biography directly from the Apostle Peter and was very careful in his writing. For those and other reasons discussed earlier, we know the Gospels constitute reliable historical reporting.

The kind of scholarly nonsense we find in skeptical endeavors like the influential "Jesus Seminar" is all too common today, and despite its consequences in the lives of the uninformed, believer or unbeliever, only serves to discredit the skeptic's own credibility and make plain his prejudices.[171] When we read the Gospels—

Matthew, Mark, Luke, and John—we are, in fact, reading what Jesus Himself actually said and did. So, what did Jesus claim? As you read the words of Jesus, ask yourself, What sort of man would say them?

> I am the light of the world. Whoever follows me will never walk in darkness, but will have the light of life (John 8:12).

> I am the resurrection and the life. He who believes in Me will live, even though he dies (John 11:25).

> For the bread of God is he who comes down from heaven and gives life to the world...I am the bread of life (John 6:33,35).

> "I tell you the truth," Jesus answered, "before Abraham was born, I am!" (John 8:58).

> When a man believes in me, he does not believe in me only, but in the one who sent me. When he looks at me, he sees the one who sent me (John 12:44-45).

> You call me "Teacher" and "Lord," and rightly so, for that is what I am (John 13:13).

> And if I go and prepare a place for you, I will come back and take you to be with me that you also may be where I am (John 14:3).

> I have overcome the world (John 16:33).

> My teaching is not my own. It comes from him who sent me. If anyone chooses to do God's will, he will find out whether my teaching comes from God or whether I speak on my own (John 7:16-17).

> I and the Father are one (John 10:30).

> All that belongs to the Father is mine (John 16:15).

> You are from below, I am from above; you are of this world, I am not of this world (John 8:23).

So startling are Jesus' claims that a natural response is to suspect Jesus was actually mad. How would anyone feel if someone else, a friend or stranger, started making such claims? But what did Jesus declare of such unbelievable, brazen assertions? Only that, "My testimony is valid" (John 8:14), and "I am the one I claim to be" (John 8:24), and "You are right in saying I am a king. In fact, for this reason I was born, and for this I came into the world, to testify to the truth. Everyone on the side of truth listens to me" (John 18:37). As we will see, these claims make no sense at all unless the Christian explanation of Jesus is true.

Throughout history, possibly three billion people have believed these claims are true. But even those in the first century who knew Jesus personally, or critically examined His claims, believed them true. Considering the astonishing nature of such assertions, perhaps that is the most amazing thing. Indeed, it would seem a miracle, or at least something very strange, if those claims were false and yet billions have believed them—as if much of humanity itself had gone mad, incapable of identifying someone plainly psychotic. Consider these testimonies:

The Apostle John wrote, "This is the disciple who testifies to these things [about Jesus] and who wrote them down. We know that his testimony is true" (John 21:24).

The physician Luke wrote, "I myself have carefully investigated everything from the beginning...so that you may know the certainty of the things you have been taught." And later, "After his [Jesus'] suffering, he showed himself to these men [apostles] and gave many convincing proofs that he was alive. He appeared to them over a period of forty days and spoke about the kingdom of God" (Luke 1:3,4; Acts 1:3).

Former skeptic and Jewish leader, Saul of Tarsus, who became the Apostle Paul, told King Herod Agrippa II that though he formerly persecuted believers in Christ, condemning them to death (Acts 26:9-11), Jesus had now personally appeared to him, confirming Jesus' resurrection and messiahship (verses 12-18). Paul then said, appealing to fulfilled prophecy and eyewitness testimony: "I stand here and testify to small and great alike. I am saying nothing beyond what the prophets and Moses said would happen...What I am saying is true and reasonable. The king is familiar with these things, and I can speak freely to him. I am convinced that none of this has escaped his notice, because it was not done in a corner" (Acts 26:22, 25b-26).

The Apostle Peter wrote, "We did not follow cleverly invented stories when we told you about the power and coming of our Lord Jesus Christ, but we were eyewitnesses of his majesty" (2 Peter 1:16).

Significantly, unlike any other religious leader, Jesus frequently appealed to His ability to *prove* His claims by predicting the future or performing spectacular miracles such as healing those born blind or raising the dead: "I am telling you now before it happens, so that when it does happen you will believe that I am He" (John 13:19). "Believe me when I say that I am in the Father and the Father is in me; or at least believe on the evidence of the miracles themselves" (John 14:11).

Philip Yancey is one of the great contemporary Christian writers and the author of two important books relevant to our discussion, *What's So Amazing about Grace?* and *The Jesus I Never Knew.* The latter title is one of the best books on Jesus, and it uncovers the truth that in our culture most people never know the real Jesus; they only know the popularized version. For example, most people tend to place Him in the same category as other great religious leaders and prophets. They assume Jesus was little different from the rest. The real Jesus is quite unlike most conceptions of Him—"ingenious, creative, challenging, fearless, compassionate, unpredictable"—and always extremely satisfying. Yancey is correct when he says, "No one who meets Jesus ever stays the same." We will not seek to present Yancey's material, as that would do it an injustice, but we will clearly show who Jesus is.

How do we determine who Jesus really is and whether or not He truly is the person of paramount importance He claims to be? The only way is to frankly examine His claims and explore the quality of the evidence that exists to support them. It is our hope that this section will help our readers understand the real Jesus Christ, for few things in life are more vital.

There are at least seven key things the Bible teaches about Jesus Christ. These stand alone, and in no other religion on earth do we find anything similar:

1. Jesus is the prophesied Messiah who was predicted hundreds of years in advance through very specific prophecies. In no other person of history can we see his life and nature prophetically outlined 400 to 1000 years before his birth.

2. Jesus is unique in all creation; in all history and religion there has never been another like Him. No other man, let alone an itinerant Jewish carpenter, born into scandal, accused of sedition, and crucified as a criminal, ever changed the world the way this man did.

3. Jesus is virgin born, and morally perfect—sinless. The world has never known any other virgin born and truly sinless person—of no other individual this world has known is it possible to differentiate between their birth and origin or to speculate over their nature.

4. Jesus is deity, the only incarnation of God there is or will be. No other man ever claimed to be God and convinced over a billion people in the twenty-first century that he was telling the truth.

5. Jesus is the world's only Savior, who died for our sins on the cross and offers eternal salvation as an entirely free gift. No one else ever claimed he would die for man's sin and that he, personally, could freely offer eternal life to all humanity.

6. Jesus rose from the dead as proof of His claims and ascended into heaven. In no other man do we find the daring to specifically predict on many occasions his own time and method of death (to the very day) or to predict his rising from the dead (to the very day), and then do it.

7. Jesus is the Final Judge; He will return on the Last Day and personally judge every person who has ever lived. No man ever said he would visibly return from heaven to judge the world and decide the eternal fate of every person who ever lived.

---

21

---

## IS JESUS THE PROPHESIED MESSIAH PREDICTED CENTURIES IN ADVANCE IN THE OLD TESTAMENT?

Messianic prophecies extend over a period of 1000 years and are given in specific detail. The first Messianic prophecy was written in the first book of the Bible (Genesis 3:15, written in approximately 1450 B.C.), and the final Messianic prophecy in the last book of the Old Testament (Malachi 4:5, written approximately 430 B.C.). In *The Case for Jesus the Messiah: Incredible Prophecies That Prove God Exists*, we discuss more than a dozen of these prophecies at length, proving that only Jesus Christ fulfills them, and therefore, that only He is the predicted Jewish Messiah (see John 5:46). For example, in the anguished imagery of King David's prayers, Psalm 22 accurately describes a crucifixion—yet this description is given hundreds of years before the method of execution by crucifixion existed. How is that possible? This Psalm was also written 1000 years before Jesus was ever born. How is that possible? No other Psalm fits the description of Christ's crucifixion better than Psalm 22; that is why it is the most frequently quoted Psalm by New Testament writers. Significantly, Jesus quoted the first verse of this Psalm while on the cross. Whatever one thinks of this Psalm, no one can deny that it describes what happened to Jesus on the cross an entire millennium later. For example, "They have pierced my hands and my feet. I can count all my bones; people stare and gloat over me. They divide my garments among them and cast lots for my clothing" (Psalm 22:16-18; see Matthew 27:35).

In Isaiah 9:6-7, written 700 years before Christ, the prophecy of the coming Messiah concerns a child to be born who will also be God and who will have an everlasting kingdom. In the Gospels, Jesus claimed that He was that incarnate God and that He would have an everlasting kingdom, proving it by rising from the dead (Matthew 16:28; 26:64; Luke 22:29-30; John 6:38-40,62; 8:42; 10:30, 36-38; 18:36; see also 2 Peter 1:11).

In Isaiah 53:3-12, we find a most amazing prophecy, one that has even converted many skeptical Jews to faith in Jesus as their true Messiah. The Messiah will be crushed and pierced for our transgressions; God will lay upon Him the iniquity of all mankind; He will bear the sin of many; and He will be assigned a grave with the wicked and with the rich in his death. The description fits Jesus in His life and atoning role so perfectly that even non-Christians can see Christ in Isaiah 53. But how is it they can see Him so clearly in something written 700 years before He was born? The prophecy is so specific that the first inclination of most people is to see it as a fraud written after the fact. But this is impossible because everyone agrees Isaiah was written in 700 B.C.—except some critics who, as with Daniel, late date it against all the evidence to help preserve their skepticism. In the Gospels, Jesus claims to fulfill this prophecy (Matthew 20:28; 26:28; Isaiah 53:12) and proves it with His resurrection. In fact, Jesus repeatedly claimed He was the predicted Messiah by continually claiming He was fulfilling Old Testament prophecies: "You diligently study the Scriptures because you think that by them you possess eternal life. These are the Scriptures that testify about me" (John 5:39; see also Matthew 26:24,54,56; Luke 24:25–27,44).

In Daniel 9:24-27, written 500 years before Christ is born, the Messiah is prophesied to be killed at the same time Jesus Himself is put to death, perhaps to the very day.[172]

In Zechariah 12:10, also written 500 years before Christ, is a prophecy that God Himself will be pierced by the inhabitants of

Jerusalem, who will mourn over Him. The Hebrew word means pierced as with a spear; Jesus was pierced by the Roman spear during His crucifixion and others mourned over Him (John 19:34-37). What is interesting about this prophecy is that God, who is Spirit (John 4:24), cannot be physically pierced; therefore this prophecy must refer to an incarnation of God, which is what Jesus claimed for Himself.

Whatever one's view of the Old Testament, one fact is unassailable: The Septuagint, the Greek translation of the entire Hebrew Scriptures, was completed by 247 B.C. Therefore, even critics must acknowledge that the hundreds of Messianic prophecies were in existence at least 250 years before Christ was born. Jesus is the only Person who has fulfilled all of these prophecies, and there is no way to avoid this fact. Old Testament scholars Delitzsch and Gloag were correct when they wrote long ago:

> So far as we can determine, these prophecies refer to the Messiah only, and cannot be predicated of another. The ancient Jews admit the Messianic character of most of them; although the modern Jews, in consequence of their controversy with the Christians, have attempted to explain them away by applications which must appear to every candid reader to be unnatural...these and other predictions have received their accomplishment in Jesus of Nazareth...the combination of prophecies is sufficient to prove that Jesus is the Messiah...[173]

Remember, in John 4:25-26 and Mark 14.61-62, Jesus Himself undeniably claimed He was the prophesied Messiah. In order to disprove this claim, one only need find a single prophecy (out of all in the Old Testament) that proves Jesus was wrong. Because no one has done this, and because Jesus filled all of the prophecies relating to His incarnation, and because He resurrected from the dead, no one can logically deny that He was and is the prophesied Jewish Messiah.

---

22

---

## WAS JESUS VIRGIN BORN AND SINLESS?

*Before they came together, she was found to be with child through the Holy Spirit.*

Matthew 1:18

What an amazing teaching is the virgin birth—yet one essential to the incarnation. Some people scoff at the idea of Jesus' virgin birth. But the virgin birth of Christ is one of the most crucial doctrines of Christianity. If Jesus were not virgin born, there would be no Christianity. First, if Jesus is not virgin born, then He was born just like every other man. This would prove He was only a man, His claim to be God incarnate was a lie, and He was self-deceived. Someone so deceived in this manner would be seriously ill and would never have had a great and positive impact on the world.

Further, if Christ was not virgin born, neither could He have been the Savior of the world. As a man, He would have inherited a sinful nature from His parents. And if He Himself were sinful, He could not have been an atoning sacrifice for the sins of the world (1 John 2:2). If He were only a man, how could His sacrifice on the cross, the sacrifice of a mere finite being, satisfy the infinite justice of a holy God offended by human sin and evil? Therefore, the virgin birth not only undergirds the doctrine of Christ's deity, it also undergirds the doctrine of Christ's sinlessness and His role as the world's Savior. This is why the virgin birth of Christ is an absolutely essential doctrine.

But does the Bible clearly teach that Jesus was born of a virgin? Isaiah 7:14, written 700 years before Christ was born, prophesies, "Therefore the Lord Himself will give you a sign: The virgin will be with child and give birth to a son, and will call him Immanuel." The word Immanuel means "God with us," an allusion to the incarnation. When Matthew describes the birth of Christ from the

Virgin Mary, he declares this prophecy of Isaiah was fulfilled in Jesus: "All this took place to fulfill what the Lord has said through the prophet [Isaiah]: The virgin [*parthenos*] will be with child and will give birth to a son, and they will call Him 'Immanuel'— which means, 'God with us'" (Matthew 1:22-23). The Greek word *parthenos* has only one meaning: virgin.

Because Jesus was virgin born, He was also sinless. He even challenged His own enemies to prove otherwise—"Can any of you prove me guilty of sin?" (John 8:46). In John 7:18 Jesus said, "He who speaks on his own does so to gain honor for himself, but he who works for the honor of the one who sent him is a man of truth; there is nothing false about him." The apostles who lived intimately with Jesus for three years were able to examine His life in critical detail. Their unanimous confession was that Jesus was sinless. The Apostle Peter said "He committed no sin" (1 Peter 2:22). The Apostle John said, "And in Him is no sin" (1 John 3:5). Even the former skeptic, the Apostle Paul, referred to Jesus as "him who had no sin" (2 Corinthians 5:21). The author of Hebrews said that Jesus was "holy, blameless, pure, set apart from sinners" as well as "one who has been tempted in every way, just as we are— yet was without sin" (Hebrews 4:15; 7:26). The Roman governor Pilate, after examining Jesus, said he could find no fault in Him (John 18:38 kjv; Matthew 27:23-25; Luke 23:13-16). Herod concluded the same. Judas himself, who betrayed Him, confessed, "I have sinned, for I have betrayed innocent blood" (Matthew 27:4).

No one can logically deny reliable eyewitness testimony and other evidence that shows Jesus is the only perfect and sinless man who ever lived. But the implications are not small. As Bishop William Quayle noted, "The calm assumption of Jesus that He is not a sinner will take hold of the wrists of any thoughtful mind and twist them till it must come to its knees." To be without sin means one is incapable of lying or deceiving others. Being sinless means Jesus was incapable of having any kind of unethical attitude or act. Nor could He have any ersatz philosophical bias because He could always and only proclaim the truth. If Jesus was sinless, then logically, what He said about Himself must be true. And if He was perfect and sinless, shouldn't we assume that what He has to say is important to us also, regardless of what we may now think about Him?

---

### 23

## IS JESUS THE ONLY INCARNATION OF GOD THERE WILL BE?

*The high-minded man must care more for the truth than for what people think.*

Aristotle

In what other religion do we find an incarnation like that of Jesus—or even an incarnation at all? At best, there is the idolatrous religion of Jainism which claims, unconvincingly, an incarnation (from a polytheistic heaven) of its god and founder, Mahavira. But, in fact, Mahavira himself denied theism and condemned the practice of praying to or even having discussions about God. The only other shadow of the biblical concept of incarnation is found in Hinduism, but here the incarnations are of mythical gods, forever cyclical, and just as forever irrelevant. According to the influential advaita school of Vedanta, the Hindu gods' incarnations are, finally, also part of the duality and *maya* (illusion) of the creation and thus never redemptive in the sense of a propitiatory atonement, or ultimately in any sense. There is no concept of incarnation in Buddhist belief unless we consider the later Mahayanist belief of an alleged Buddha nature, supposedly inherent in all men, to be an "incarnation" of a mythically deified Buddha. Judaism has no incarnation; in Judaism the idea of Jesus as the incarnate Son of God is adamantly rejected. Taoism has only an impersonal principle, the Tao, as an ultimate reality and no need or place for an incarnation. In Sikhism, Guru Nanak taught that God is unborn and non-incarnated; in Parsism (Zoroastrianism) the god Ahura Mazda is not incarnated; and in Islam the thought of an incarnation is utterly blasphemous. In Confucianism, Confucius acknowledged himself as only a sinful man. Although he was later worshiped, he was never incarnate. Of the 11 or 12 classical world religions, there is no concept of incarnation except in Jainism and Hinduism, and both of those involve myths.

Only Christianity can claim an incarnation. In the sober words of G. K. Chesterton, the incarnation of Christ "makes nothing but dust and nonsense of comparative religion."[174] Thus, Chesterton was right when he asserted that only the Apostles have good news for the rest of the world: "Nobody else except those messengers has any Gospel; nobody else has any good news, for the simple reason that nobody else has any news."[175]

---

## 24

## IS JESUS THE WORLD'S ONLY PROVEN SAVIOR WHO DIED FOR OUR SINS ON THE CROSS AND WHO OFFERS ETERNAL SALVATION AS A WHOLLY FREE GIFT?

*Jesus Christ is the center of all, and the goal toward which all tends.*

**Blaise Pascal**

In spite of the many claims by people today that there are many "saviors," many "gurus," and many paths to God, Christianity teaches that Jesus alone is the way to God. Why?

Jesus Himself taught that only He was the way to God, and there is no greater authority than Jesus. If Jesus was correct when He said, "All authority in heaven and on earth has been given to me" (Matthew 28:18), then no other option remains. It's not a matter of what we might personally wish to believe; it's a matter of what is true.

Jesus declared, "I am the way and the truth and the life. No one comes to the Father except through me" (John 14:6). He emphasized, "I tell you the truth, I am the gate for the sheep...I am the gate; whoever enters through me will be saved...I have come that they may have life, and have it to the full. I am the good shepherd. The good shepherd lays down his life for the sheep" (John 10:7-11). Jesus clearly claimed that He was an atoning sacrifice for the world's sin when He said, "the Son of Man did not come to be served, but to serve, and to give his life as a ransom for many" (Matthew 20:28), and "This is my blood of the covenant, which is poured out for many for the forgiveness of sins" (Matthew 26:28).

Because Jesus is the only incarnation of God, and He is God's only Son, when He died on the cross for human sin, He became the only possible way of salvation for men and women. In other words, no one else paid the penalty of divine justice against human sin. This is why the Bible teaches, "Salvation is found in no one else, for there is no other name under heaven given to men by which we must be saved" (Acts 4:12). Further, "This is good, and pleases God our Savior, who wants all men to be saved and to come to a knowledge of the truth. For there is one God and one mediator between God and men, the man Christ Jesus, who gave Himself as a ransom for all men—the testimony given in its proper time" (1 Timothy 2:3-6).

In addition, Christ offers a salvation unlike that in any other religion. Forgiveness of sins and eternal life are freely given without cost to the recipient. Indeed, Jesus claimed that He would personally raise all the dead and give eternal life to those who had believed on Him: "For my Father's will is that everyone who looks to the Son and believes in him shall have eternal life, and I will raise him up at the last day" (John 6:40). "For just as the Father raises the dead and gives them life, even so the Son gives life to whom he is pleased to give it" (John 5:21). "I tell you the truth, whoever hears my word and believes him who sent me has eternal life and will not be condemned; he has crossed over from death to life" (John 5:24). "I tell you the truth, he who believes has everlasting life" (John

6:47). "This righteousness from God comes through faith in Jesus Christ to all who believe. There is no difference, for all have sinned and fall short of the glory of God, and are justified freely by his grace through redemption that came by Christ Jesus" (Romans 3:22-24). "He saved us, not because of righteous things we had done, but because of his mercy" (Titus 3:5).

In all history, nothing like this has ever been proclaimed outside biblical Christianity.

## 25

## DID JESUS ACTUALLY RISE FROM THE DEAD?

We often hear so much about Christ being risen from the dead that we don't appreciate the enormity of it. Everyone knows that people do not rise from the dead. Just consider the extraordinary commotion that would be generated if President John F. Kennedy actually came back from the dead and was seen by his closest friends and family, plus 500 Democrats and some skeptical reporters as well, for weeks on end.

It would change the world.

Since no one rises from the dead, the fact that Christianity has become the world's dominant religion based entirely on such a claim is stunning. Somehow it has to be explained.

How do we *know* Jesus rose from the dead? We will discuss this in more detail shortly, but to whet the appetite, let us preface the discussion with a few observations. First, hundreds of millions of people—including scientists, intellectuals, former skeptics, and leading lawyers throughout history and today—have all concluded that the evidence for the truth of Christianity and its view of Jesus and His resurrection is persuasive, even compelling. Where else in the history of religion do we see this: an incredible supernatural event that is widely investigated and accepted by people of such influence?

Second, before any of the events had occurred, Jesus made no less than ten specific predictions about His death and resurrection, all of which came true. These predictions are obviously unique in religion and, if they were false, would never have been remembered, let alone written about. If Jesus didn't rise, everyone would have known it.

Third, even critics agree Jesus was crucified and died at Roman hands and that the location of His tomb was public knowledge. Nor can anyone logically deny that a one- to two-ton stone was rolled over the face of the grave. A highly trained Roman military guard[176] was set at the grave to prevent anyone from stealing the body. But almost everyone agrees, critics included, that the tomb was found empty Sunday morning.

Fourth, no other theory to explain this fact has ever proved satisfactory except the Christian one. No credible alternative exists—in fact other explanations are more incredible than the resurrection, as we will later see.

Fifth, there were numerous resurrection appearances of Christ after His death. He appeared to many different people—to disciples who did not believe it at first, to a crowd of 500, and to selected individuals. He appeared to them in many different ways, locations, and circumstances. These appearances eventually compelled belief, despite skepticism, as the accounts reveal.

In fact, when the Apostle Paul wrote that over 500 people had personally seen Jesus alive, all at the same time, he was, in effect, throwing down a gauntlet to skeptics. 500 people? That is utterly preposterous unless true. What if I (Weldon) called the *New York Times* tomorrow to claim that 500 people, all at the same time, had seen President Kennedy alive, that he had also appeared to his family members and even to others who were incredulous after hearing such reports, that the reports were consistent, and that sober people claimed to see him for a month and a half? No sane person would make such an outlandish claim unless he was absolutely sure of three things: 1) it really happened, 2) family members would testify they saw him, and 3) those 500 people would personally corroborate what was said.

Further, Paul's mention of the 500 witnesses appears in the "earliest and best-authenticated passage of all."[177] Indeed, German historian Hans von Campenhausen declared, "this account meets all the demands of historical reliability that could possibly be made of such a text" and more impressive, perhaps the greatest living systematic theologian in the world, Wolfhart Pannenberg, threw skeptical German theology for a loop by basing "his entire theology [!] precisely on the historical evidence of the resurrection of Jesus as supplied in Paul's list of appearances" where this statement about 500 witnesses occurs.[178]

As former atheist Lee Strobel recalls of his own skeptical investigation into the resurrection, "All of the gospel and Acts evidence—incident after incident, witness after witness, detail after detail, corroboration on top of corroboration—was extremely impressive. Although I tried, I couldn't think of any more thoroughly attested event in ancient history."[179] And as one familiar with legal evidence, he points out that if we were to call every witness to the resurrection into a court of law for cross-examination of just fifteen minutes each, doing this nonstop Monday through Friday, eight hours a day, it would take three full weeks plus overtime—129 straight hours—to hear all the eyewitness testimony. After listening to credible eyewitnesses eight hours a day, for sixteen days, under cross-examination, who could walk away unconvinced that Jesus had risen from the dead?[180] When enough witnesses say the same thing, time and again, over and over, and there is no contrary evidence presented anywhere by anyone, a case must be considered established.

As exceptional as the resurrection is, it doesn't take a rocket scientist to conclude that if Christ died (and everyone agrees He did) and if He was seen alive by large numbers of credible eyewitnesses (and this can neither be logically nor convincingly doubted), then He rose from the dead! Indeed, the very existence of the Christian religion is itself proof of the resurrection. Why?

Because, as we will show later, apart from the resurrection, the Christian religion would not exist.

If Jesus is the only man to rise from the dead, who can possibly ignore Him? As Dr. D.A. Carson, whose Ph.D. in New Testament is from Cambridge University, remarks, "the resurrection was the ultimate vindication of his identity."[181]

---

### 26

## IS JESUS THE FINAL JUDGE, THE ONE WHO WILL DRAMATICALLY RETURN TO EARTH ON THE LAST DAY AND JUDGE EVERY PERSON WHO HAS EVER LIVED?

*The modern world, because it is indifferent to dogmatic truth, has logically become indifferent to ethical truth.*
Bertrand L. Conway

*Pure truth, like pure gold, has been found unfit for circulation, because men have discovered that it is far more convenient to adulterate the truth than to refine themselves.*
Charles Caleb Colton

No man can convincingly claim to determine the eternal destiny of his fellow creatures, but this is just what Jesus claimed. Because Jesus is God, and because He is the very one who died for the world's sin, He is the one who will judge each man and woman who has ever lived and make the final determination of each one's destiny, as He said:

> Moreover, the Father judges no one, but has entrusted all judgment to the Son, that all may honor the Son just as they honor the Father. He who does not honor the Son does not honor the Father, who sent Him...a time is coming when all who are in their graves will hear [My] voice and come out—those who have done good will rise

to live, and those who have done evil will rise to be condemned (John 5:22-29).

Jesus also taught,

> When the Son of Man comes in his glory, and all the angels with him, he will sit on his throne in heavenly glory. All the nations will be gathered before him, and he will separate the people one from another as a shepherd separates the sheep from the goats. He will put the sheep on His right and goats on His left. Then the King will say to those on His right, "Come, you who are blessed by my Father; take your inheritance, the kingdom prepared for you since the creation of the world..." Then He will say to those on his left, "Depart from me, you who are cursed, into the eternal fire prepared for the devil and his angels"...Then they will go away to eternal punishment, but the righteous to eternal life (Matthew 25:31-34,41,46).

Proof of this coming judgment can be found in Christ's resurrection: "In the past God overlooked such ignorance, but now he commands all people everywhere to repent. For he has set a day when he will judge the world with justice by the man he has appointed. He has given proof of this to all men by raising him from the dead" (Acts 17:30-31).

In light of this, we might wish to consider the well noted "wager" of Blaise Pascal the eminent mathematician (the computer language Pascal is named after him), physicist, and genius, which is basically an argument of logical self-preservation. God either exists or not, and we must of necessity lay odds for or against Him. If I wager for Him and He does not exist, there is no loss. If I wager for Him and He exists, there is infinite gain. If I wager against Him and He does not exist, there is neither loss nor gain. But if I wager against Him and He exists, there is infinite loss. There is a single hypothesis where I am exposed to the loss of everything. Wisdom, therefore, instructs me to make the wager which ensures my winning all or, at worst, losing nothing.

If the Christian God does not exist, then because of its positive teachings, nothing is lost by embracing Christianity. But if God does exist and I believe, I gain everything in eternal life. Of course, if God exists and I reject Him, then everything is forfeited in an eternal hell. Pascal may have had Jesus' teaching in mind: "What good will it be for a man if he gains the whole world, yet forfeits his soul? What can a man give in exchange for his soul?" (Matthew 16:26-27). Unfortunately, there will be nothing worse for the unbeliever if Christianity turns out to be true.

If Jesus is God incarnate and rose from the dead as proof of His claims, then one wonders, Who will escape a personal appointment with Him at death? At that moment, each of us will face Him as either Savior or Judge. It's not an issue of what anyone believes; it's entirely an issue of who Jesus is.

---

### 27

### IS IT POSSIBLE TO *KNOW* THAT JESUS REALLY IS WHO HE CLAIMED TO BE?

*Truth is tough. It will not break, like a bubble, at a touch; nay, you may kick it about all day like a football, and it will be round and full at evening.*
**Oliver Wendell Holmes, Sr.**

There are only four logical choices we have concerning Jesus Christ. As we examine the following material, the reader should decide for himself the one option most likely to be true:

1. He was a fraud.
2. He was mentally ill.
3. He was invented.
4. He was God.

There are no other options we can think of. As we proceed to examine these alternatives, we shall demonstrate that the fourth option is the only one that any open-minded, thinking person can reasonably arrive at.

## Was Jesus a Fraud?

As far as we know, hardly anyone of sound mind has seriously maintained that Christ was a fraud—a liar and deceiver—even among the most fanatical atheists. Jesus' ethical teachings are the highest mankind has, and His personal moral character is above reproach. Even His enemies could not convict Him of sin, dishonesty, or deceit.

It is morally impossible that someone of the highest ethical character would knowingly deceive people concerning the most vital aspect of his teaching—his own identity. Even the great nineteenth-century British historian, W.E.H. Lecky, a committed opponent of organized Christianity, wrote the following sentiments about Jesus, which have been repeated many times over the centuries by men of all and no religious persuasion. In his *History of European Morals from Augustus to Charlemagne*, he wrote,

> It was reserved for Christianity to present to the world an ideal character which through all the changes of eighteen centuries has inspired the hearts of men with an impassioned love; has shown itself capable of acting on all ages, nations, temperaments and conditions; has been not only the highest pattern of virtue, but the strongest incentive to its practice, and has exerted so deep an influence, that it may be truly said, that the simple record of three short years of active life has done more to regenerate and to soften mankind, than all the disquisitions of philosophers and than all the exhortations of moralists.[182]

Who, then, can imagine that Jesus deliberately lied concerning His own nature? And is it possible that a man of such noble character and exemplary moral persuasion would frequently claim He would rise from the dead, knowing this was also a lie? Contemporary philosopher and theologian Dr. John Warwick Montgomery asserts, "To answer anything but an unqualified 'No' is to renounce sound ethical judgment."[183]

Dr. Philip Schaff was considered America's finest church historian. He also edited the impressive *Schaff-Herzog Encyclopedia of Religious Knowledge*. He argues,

> How, in the name of logic, common sense, and experience, could an imposter—that is a deceitful, selfish, depraved man—have invented, and consistently maintained from the beginning to end, the purest and noblest character known in history with the most perfect air of truth and reality?"[184]

Further, James Sire, author of *Why Should Anyone Believe Anything at All?*, offers other reasons to reject this option:

> There is simply no evidence that Jesus did not think He was telling the truth...When liars elaborate or answer the same kinds of questions repeatedly, they are easily caught in inconsistencies. There is in Jesus a unity of teaching: the stories, the clever sayings, the constant compassion for people, the obvious wisdom of His teaching, the ethical depth of both His teaching and His character. No fault could be found in Him...If He was lying, He...would be no better than the worst religious huckster we know of today, no better than Bhagwan Shree Rajneesh or Jim Jones or David Koresh. No one can call the Jesus of the Gospels that kind of bad man. It fits with none of the evidence whatsoever...[Critics argue] Maybe Jesus was right about a lot of things...but wrong about who He was...The problem here is that this kind of delusion is no small matter.[185]

No one can logically maintain Jesus was a fraud, liar, and deceiver. Alternative one is ruled out.

### Was Jesus Deluded?

Our second option is even more difficult to believe. Was Jesus self-deluded, mentally ill, or psychotic? For someone to be convinced that he is God when he is only a man is the height of psychosis. Mental illness or psychosis is defined as an inability to identify reality and to distinguish it from fantasy. The fifth edition of *Introduction to Psychology* describes psychosis as follows:

> The psychotic has to some extent given up [his personal] struggle [to cope with reality] and lost contact with reality. He may withdraw into his own fantasy world frequently; his thought processes are disturbed to the extent that he experiences delusions (false beliefs) or hallucinations.[186]

But what insane man could ever deliver a self-portrait and teachings that are the epitome of sanity and mental health? Former skeptic Lee Strobel, an award-winning journalist with a master's degree from Yale Law School, concluded his own study with this:

> I could detect no sign of dementia, delusions, or paranoia. On the contrary, I was moved once more by his profound wisdom, his uncanny insights, his poetic eloquence, and his deep compassion. Historian Philip Schaff said it better than I can. "Is such an intellect—clear as the sky, bracing as the mountain air, sharp and penetrating as a sword, thoroughly healthy and vigorous, always ready and always self-possessed—liable to a radical and most serious delusion concerning his own character and mission? *Preposterous imagination!*[187]

Psychiatrist J. T. Fisher observes,

> If you were to take the sum total of all authoritative articles ever written by the most qualified of psychologists and psychiatrists on the subject of mental hygiene, if you were to combine them and refine them and cleave out the excess verbiage...and if you were to have the unadulterated bits of pure scientific knowledge concisely expressed by the most capable of living poets, you would have an awkward and incomplete summation of the Sermon on the Mount. And it would suffer immeasurably through comparison...Here rests the blueprint for successful human life with optimum mental health and contentment.[188]

Dr. Montgomery explains:

> But one cannot very well have it both ways: if Jesus' teachings provide "the blueprint for successful human life with optimum mental health," then the teacher cannot be a lunatic who totally misunderstands the nature of his own personality. Note the absolute dichotomy: if the documentary records of Jesus' life are accurate, and Jesus was not a charlatan, then he was either God incarnate as he claimed or a psychotic. If we cannot take the latter alternative (and, considering its consequences, who really can follow this path to its logical conclusion?), we must arrive at a Jesus who claimed to be God incarnate simply because he was God.[189]

No man can logically maintain Jesus was deluded or psychotic. No one who reads His words and carefully examines His clarity of thought, incisive argumentation, or penetrating insight into human nature can possibly think so. Alternative two is ruled out.

### Was Jesus Invented?

Our third option is the least credible of all. Everyone but a few diehard atheists agree that Jesus was no invention. No less an authority than the *Encyclopædia Britannica* points out, "These independent accounts prove that in ancient times even the opponents of Christianity never doubted the historicity of Jesus, which was disputed for the first time and on inadequate grounds by several authors at the end of the 18th, during the 19th, and at the beginning of the 20th centuries."[190]

This theory requires that the disciples falsely invented Jesus' teachings and lied about His resurrection. Such men must be classified as deceivers or crazy. But this is impossible because as we will see later, the disciples had neither the motive nor the ability to invent Jesus, nor did they act in any way other than honestly. Their strict Jewish ethical code and moral character would have prevented such conspiratorial deception. The writers of the New Testament and the earliest Christians were so resolutely committed to the truth that we find the words "truth," "true," and related words appearing some 366 times in the New Testament! Noted theologian Dr. Carl F. Henry, after several years of research and study at Cambridge University, authored the impressive six-volume *God, Revelation and Authority* in which he defended the truth of Christianity, the inerrancy of the Scriptures, etc. As noted earlier, after a lifetime of study he concluded, "Truth is Christianity's most enduring asset."[191]

As Pascal pointed out,

> The supposition that the apostles were impostors is very absurd. Let us think it out. Let us imagine those twelve men, assembled after the death of Jesus Christ, plotting to say that He was risen....The apostles were either deceived or deceivers. Either supposition has difficulties; for it is not possible to mistake a man raised from the dead.[192]

The idea that some ancient fishermen and a few followers sat down and, for some incomprehensible reason, decided to invent a character so unique, superlative, and transcendent that He surpasses the finest efforts of the best writers in every age is ridiculous. *No one* could invent such a man. Historian Philip Schaff argues,

> A character so original, so complete, so uniformly consistent, so perfect, so human and yet so high above all human greatness, can be neither a fraud nor a fiction. The poet, as has been well said, would in this case be greater than the hero. It would take more than a Jesus to invent a Jesus.[193]

It is not possible that the person of Jesus could ever have been manufactured or invented. Alternative three is ruled out. Only one alternative remains.

## Was Jesus God?

It is impossible to maintain that Jesus was either a liar, deceived or psychotic, or invented. Our only option is that He was God incarnate, both Lord and God. Psychologist Gary Collins, Ph.D., remarks:

Jesus didn't just claim to be God—he backed it up with amazing feats of healing, with astounding demonstrations of power over nature, with transcendent and unprecedented teaching, with divine insights into people, and ultimately with his own resurrection from the dead, which absolutely nobody else has been able to duplicate. So when Jesus claimed to be God, it wasn't crazy. It was the truth.[194]

This is why the famous Cambridge scholar C.S. Lewis concluded that

The historical difficulty of giving for the life, sayings and influence of Jesus any explanation that is not harder than the Christian explanation, is very great. The discrepancy between the depth and sanity and (let me add) shrewdness of his moral teaching and the rampant megalomania which must be behind his theological teaching unless he is indeed God, has never been satisfactorily gotten over. Hence, the non-Christian hypotheses succeed one another with the restless fertility of bewilderment.[195]

Elsewhere, Lewis expands on the idea and shows why the non-Christian really has no logical alternative but to accept that Jesus is God:

"I'm ready to accept Jesus as a great moral teacher, but I don't accept his claim to be God." That is the one thing we must not say. A man who was merely a man and said the sort of things Jesus said would not be a great moral teacher. He would either be a lunatic—on a level with the man who says he is a poached egg—or else he would be the Devil of Hell. You must make your choice. Either this man was, and is, the Son of God; or else a madman or something worse. You can shut him up for a fool, you can spit at him and kill him as a demon; or you can fall at his feet and call him Lord and God. But let us not come with any patronizing nonsense about his being a great human teacher. He has not left that open to us. He did not intend to.[196]

# The Resurrection of Christ

## 28

## What Is the Evidence for the Resurrection?

*When all treasures are tried, truth is the fairest.*
William Langland

The evidence for the resurrection can be summarized in two historical facts: 1) Jesus was publicly crucified and died. 2) A few days later, He was seen alive by many people; He engaged in a variety of physical interactions with them over a lengthy period of time in numerous locations and circumstances; and on one occasion He was seen alive by 500 people at one time.

Skeptics are correct to demand quality evidence. Did He really die, and was He really seen? From one viewpoint, it is rather amazing that hundreds of books have been written attempting to disprove one fact or the other. From another viewpoint, it's not surprising at all, given the implications for unbelief. We tend to think that these hundreds of books would never have been written in the first place unless the case were quite strong to begin with. Scholars preoccupied with so many other things will rarely take the time to write against obvious falsehoods.

Proving the resurrection is actually quite simple; getting people to believe it is another matter.

We know the Gospels constitute accurate historical reporting, and of Christ's numerous miracles, the resurrection receives the most extensive coverage by far. If the Gospels are historically accurate, then the most carefully documented event in the Gospels must also be considered accurate.[197]

It is also important to understand the unique nature of the situation. Whoever said he would come back from the dead after being publicly executed? Consider the Pope publicly declaring that he would shortly be executed as a criminal but would rise from the dead three days later. What if the president of the United States made such a claim? Because we would know the chances of their prediction actually happening would be zero, we would know they were either deluded or lying. Sane people never make astounding claims they know they cannot possibly fulfill. But Jesus made such impossible-sounding claims on numerous occasions (Matthew 12:39-40; 16:21; 17:9, 22-23; 20:17-19; 26:31-32,64; John 2:19-22).

Further, note the specific nature of Jesus' predictions:

- He would perform the resurrection by His own power

- the elders and chief priests would condemn Him to death and deliver Him to the Romans

- His persecution would happen in Jerusalem

- the Old Testament prophecies concerning the Messiah's death and resurrection would be fulfilled

- all 12 apostles would desert Him

- He would die specifically by crucifixion

- He would rise from the dead in three days

How could Jesus possibly be so specific? How did He know He would not die by natural or accidental death? How could He know He would die *by* crucifixion, *on* the Passover, *in* Jerusalem, rather than in a dozen different ways, times, or locations? How could He know He would rise on the *third* day or rise at all? Had He failed in any one of these predictions, He would have been shown to be wrong and His claim to be God proven false. Claiming to be God leaves one very few options. But Jesus was not wrong even once.

We can be brief with the historical evidence that Jesus died because almost everyone agrees He did. His death may be considered, beyond doubt, a fact of history. We know Jesus died because

- He was crucified publicly according to standard Roman practice, and survival from crucifixion was unknown

- Roman soldiers maintained a careful watch from below the cross to ensure death

- dozens of friends and enemies watched Him as He died upon the cross, and they heard His death cry

- The soldiers who came to break the legs of the other Jewish prisoners (so the prisoners would suffocate) did not break Jesus' legs because they saw He was already dead

- a Roman soldier pierced Jesus' side and heart with a spear to be sure He was dead

- Pilate had the commanding centurion reconfirm Jesus' death

- those who removed Jesus' body would have noticed any life in Him and would not have put Him in the grave

- all four Gospel writers specifically declared that Jesus died (Matthew 27:50; Mark 15:37; Luke 23:46; John 19:30)

- the book of Acts and the epistles of Paul repeat over a dozen times that Christ died

It took at least 1800 years for someone to propose the nonsense that Jesus didn't really die on the cross. No one could possibly have made such a claim on the day of the crucifixion itself.

We can also be brief in proving that the tomb was empty because this is also conceded and critics themselves have to agree Jesus' enemies were never able to produce the body. Again, many people saw Jesus die, and they knew where He was buried. Witnesses saw His body placed in the tomb, and they saw a one to two-ton stone rolled across the entrance (Matthew 27:60-61; Luke 23:55; Mark 15:46-47; John 19:41-42). They saw the placing of the Roman seal on the tomb and the Roman guards put on duty to secure it (Matthew 27:62-66). No one has ever doubted that the tomb was found empty—not even critics. However they try to explain it otherwise, every critic, and every critical theory accepts the fact of the empty tomb. The Jewish authorities never questioned the report of the guards that the tomb was empty; they knew the guards would never have come back with such a story unless it were true (Matthew 28:11-15). But due to the extreme controversy over Jesus, the Jewish authorities would have had to check the tomb for themselves and then make the most exhaustive search possible to try and find the body, which they obviously never did. Thus the earliest Jewish propaganda against the Christians presumes an empty tomb (Matthew 28:12-15). In addition, the grave cloths that had encased Jesus with 70 pounds of spices were in the shape of a cocoon as if the body had simply disappeared from within. It's no wonder the Apostle John looked into the tomb and, as it is reported, "saw and believed" (John 20:8). Finally, the remains of unparalleled religious figures are almost universally venerated—pilgrimages are made to visit their tombs. Everyone agrees that these tombs contain the bones of the great prophet or founder, but everyone also agrees that when Christians visit Christ's tomb in Israel, they go to see an empty tomb.

While there are a dozen lines of evidence for the resurrection, we will concentrate on four:

1. The appearances of Jesus to people who were skeptical and never expected it—these appearances cannot rationally be explained in any other way

2. The existence of Christianity—the Church could not possibly have begun apart from the physical resurrection of Christ

3. The testimony of skeptical and brilliant individuals that, based on the quality of the overall evidence, Christ did in fact rise from the dead

4. The inability of the remaining skeptics to offer any credible alternate theory, even with 2000 years to come up with one

If these are argued successfully, we don't think the resurrection can logically be denied by anyone.

It is important to note that virtually all the following facts would be accepted by the majority of scholars, Christian or skeptical:

1. Jesus died by crucifixion after claiming on at least a dozen occasions He would rise from the dead.

2. Jesus was buried in a public tomb of a wealthy person.

3. The death of Christ caused His followers to lose all hope in His Messianic claims.

4. The tomb was found empty.

5. The disciples had genuine experiences, which they were convinced were literal appearances of the risen Christ.

6. The disciples were radically transformed from skeptics and doubters to bold proclaimers of Christ's resurrection.

7. Eleven of the 12 apostles suffered martyrs' deaths for their convictions about the resurrection.

8. The resurrection message was absolutely central to the early preaching of the Church.

9. The resurrection message is central to the entire New Testament.

10. The resurrection was first proclaimed in the very environment most hostile to it—Jerusalem. Even there, those motivated to disprove the resurrection could not do so.

11. The Church exists only because of the disciples' conviction that the resurrection occurred.

12. The apostles Thomas and Paul, and many other skeptics, became convinced of the resurrection on the basis of what they claimed was empirical evidence.

Given these generally accepted facts, we are already not far removed from rendering a positive verdict on the resurrection.

---

### 29

## DID JESUS APPEAR ALIVE TO MANY FOLLOWERS WHO WERE SKEPTICAL?

Only the reality of Christ's physical appearances can logically explain the disciples' conversion from skepticism to belief, their claims to being eyewitnesses, and their willingness to suffer great persecution and death for those claims—arrest and incarceration in dungeons, severe flogging, and death by crucifixion. People never submit to torture and death for what they know is false—and if the resurrection weren't true, they would have known it. Indeed, the great variety of Jesus' appearances, their physical nature and other factors make disbelief in the resurrection the greater wonder. In the list below, in almost every case, the disciples both saw and heard Jesus, and in at least five cases they either touched Him, saw His death wounds, or Jesus offered to be touched, or He ate with them. In four cases, they saw the empty tomb and empty grave cloths.

## The Resurrection Appearances

1. to the women as they returned from the tomb after having seen the angel, who informed them that Christ had risen (Matthew 28:1-10)

2. to Mary Magdalene at the tomb, during her second visit to the tomb that morning (John 20:10-18; Mark 16:9-11)

3. to Peter sometime before the evening of the resurrection day but under circumstances the details of which are not given (Luke 24:34; 1 Corinthians 15:5)

4. to Cleopas and another disciple on the road to Emmaus on Easter afternoon (Luke 24:13-35; Mark 16:12-13)

5. to ten of the apostles with others whose names are not given (Thomas is absent), gathered together at their evening meal on Easter Sunday (Luke 24:36-40; John 20:19-23; Mark 16:14-18)

6. a week later to all 11 apostles, including Thomas (John 20:26-28)

7. to some of the disciples fishing at the Sea of Galilee, the time undesignated (John 21:1-23)

8. to all the apostles on a specific mountain in Galilee (Matthew 28:16-20)

9. to James, with specific information as to time and place not stated (1 Corinthians 15:7)

10. to all the apostles on the Mount of Olives at Jerusalem just prior to the ascension (Luke 24:50-52; Acts 1:3-9; Mark 16:19)

11. to 500 additional believers all at once (1 Corinthians 15:6)

12. to Paul on the Damascus road (1 Corinthians 15:8; Acts 9:1-9)[198]

All of these people were eyewitnesses to the event. The *Oxford American Dictionary* defines a witness as "a person who gives evidence in court" and as "a person who is present at an event in order to testify to the fact that it took place." The apostles did this unceasingly. Because Jesus "gave many convincing proofs that he was alive" to those who saw Him (Acts 1:3), the disciples emphasized their eyewitnesses testimony:

- we were eyewitnesses (2 Peter 1:16)

- we proclaim to you what we have seen and heard (1 John 1:1-3)

- we are all witnesses (Acts 2:32)

- we are witnesses of these things (Acts 5:32)

- you know...and we are witnesses...and solemnly testify (Acts 10:37-43 NASB)

What is sometimes overlooked however is that the disciples also followed strict Jewish law that commanded them to be truthful witnesses on penalty of divine judgment (Exodus 20:16; 23:1; Proverbs 19:5). "And if Christ has not been raised, then our preaching is vain, your faith also is vain. Moreover we are even found to be false witnesses of God, because we testified against God that he raised Christ, whom he did not raise..." (1 Corinthians 15:14-15 NASB).

Another fact often overlooked is that the disciples were not hoping for a resurrection, did not believe one would occur, had given up on Jesus, and in truth, were skeptical when they began hearing reports that He had risen. Some continued to doubt *even when* they saw Him. The disciples were expecting anything but a resurrection. In fact, for the disciples, crucifixion meant Jesus had been cursed of God. (This was actually true, but not in the manner they then thought.) And if He was cursed of God, He could not possibly have been their Messiah: "But we had hoped that he was the one who was going to redeem Israel" (Luke 24:21). There was no hope remaining, no motive to continue. His followers became depressed and dejected. So how did they change? Nothing but the resurrection could have changed their interpretation of Jesus being cursed of God, with all the terrible implications. Can we really believe that the mental frame of mind of the disciples prior to the resurrection appearances was sufficient to "invent" the Church? Could the unbelieving and skeptical disciples have proclaimed a resurrection when they never expected it in the first place? As Dr. Norval Geldenhuys observes: "It is historically and psychologically impossible that the followers of Jesus, who at His crucifixion were so completely despondent and perplexed, would within a few weeks thereafter enter the world (as they did) with such unheard-of joy, power and devotion, if it had not been for the fact that He had risen from the dead, had appeared to them, and had proved that His claims to be the Son of God were genuine."[199]

Indeed, almost all of these Jews later died as Christian martyrs because of their conviction that Jesus rose from the dead. Even if we thrust aside their ethical standards, the disciples were psychologically incapable of fraud. As Jews, the disciples' beliefs would have prohibited them from deifying Jesus *unless* the resurrection had already proved to them beyond doubt that Jesus actually was God incarnate.

These men, then, were not people who were ready to believe. When they first heard Jesus was resurrected, it is natural that "they did not believe...because [it] seemed to them like nonsense" (Luke 24:11). As the Gospels show, it was only after Jesus appeared to them again and again, talking with them for long periods, eating with them, encouraging them to touch Him to see that He had a physical body, showing them the wounds in His hands and His side, that they became convinced. "Look at my hands and my feet. It is I myself. Touch me and see" (Luke 24:39; see also John 20:20,27). If they *had* expected a resurrection, they would have been waiting for it. But they weren't waiting, and they needed a lot of convincing when it happened. Again, even when they saw Him some still had a hard time believing it: "And while they still did

not believe it because of joy and amazement, he asked them..."
(Luke 24:41; see also Matthew 28:17).

It is not too much to say that in some measure the disciples
were actually convinced against their will. At one time or another
Jesus rebuked all 11 apostles for their unbelief in His resurrection
(Luke 24:25-27,38). Thomas was not the only one who was a hard-
headed skeptic:

> But he [Thomas] said to them, "Unless I see the nail marks
> in his hands and put my finger where the nails were, and
> put my hand into his side, I will not believe it." A week later
> his disciples were in the house again, and Thomas was with
> them. Though the doors were locked, Jesus came and
> stood among them and said, "Peace be with you!" Then he
> said to Thomas, "Put your finger here; see my hands. Reach
> out your hand and put it into my side. Stop doubting and
> believe." Thomas said to him, "My Lord and my God."
> (John 20:24-28)

The record is also clear that none of the disciples understood
the necessity for a resurrection. This is seen both from Peter's
rebuke to Jesus when He predicted His death and resurrection
(Matthew 16:21-22) and from Christ's prediction of His resurrection after the transfiguration (Matthew 17:9, 22-23). Mark says of
the disciples, "But they did not understand this statement, and
they were afraid to ask Him" (Mark 9:32). The disciples not only
didn't believe in the resurrection, they didn't understand the
implications. After Jesus spoke of His rising from the dead "they
seized upon that statement, discussing with one another what
rising from the dead might mean" (Mark 9:10). On another occasion when Jesus spoke of His resurrection, "The disciples did not
understand any of this" (Luke 18:34). After Jesus had died, they
had no thought of carrying on His cause. A resurrection never
entered their minds—until it was thrust there, first by reports, and
then by empirical evidence they could not deny.

In other words, how do we account for the disciples coming
to wholeheartedly believe in something that was "impossible,"

completely unexpected, something even resisted—unless it really happened? We continue this theme in the next question.

30
_____

## IN WHAT WAY IS THE EXISTENCE OF THE CHRISTIAN CHURCH PROOF OF THE RESURRECTION?

Could the Christian Church have come into existence solely by the efforts of what had become, after Jesus' crucifixion and death, a group of disheartened, frightened, cynical apostles? Not in a million years. Had Jesus not resurrected, we would not have the option of discussing His identity today. Two thousand years ago His name would have dissipated once and for all into the mists of historical obscurity.

The resurrected Christ alone accounts for the existence of the Church. It can hardly be overestimated how devastating the crucifixion was to the apostles. They had sacrificed everything for Jesus, including their jobs, their homes, and their families (Matthew 19:27). Everything of value was pinned squarely on Jesus: their hopes, their lives, everything. But now He was dead, publicly branded a criminal. They had been taught by the rabbis that God would never let His Messiah suffer death, so for them, that was it. Jesus was crucified, dead, and gone—a terrible deception somehow. As Dr. Edwin Yamauchi, one of the country's leading experts in ancient history says, "Crucifixion was the most abhorrent fate that anyone could undergo, and the fact that there was a movement based on a crucified man has to be explained."[200]

In light of all this, how do we account for the beginning and remarkable expansion of the Christian church? In his 7000-page *History of the Christian Church* Dr. Philip Schaff is correct when he writes,

> The Christian church rests on the resurrection of its Founder. Without this fact the church could never have been born, or if born, it would soon have died a natural

death. The miracle of the resurrection and the existence of
Christianity are so closely connected that they must stand
or fall together...the Christian religion...is either the
greatest miracle or the greatest delusion which history
records.

Noted philosopher of religion Dr. William Lane Craig, who has
earned dual doctorates in philosophy and theology, discusses how
a mysterious "something" must be proposed to account for the
Christian church coming into existence:

It is quite clear that without the belief in the resurrection
the Christian faith could not have come into being...Now
the question becomes: What caused that belief? As R.H.
Fuller says, even the most skeptical critic must presuppose
some mysterious "X" to get the movement going. But what
was that "X?"...Clearly, it would not be the result of Christian influences, for at that time there was no Christianity...But neither can belief in the resurrection be
explained as a result of Jewish influences...The Jewish
conception of resurrection differed in two important, fundamental respects from Jesus' resurrection.

In Jewish thought the resurrection always (1) occurred
after the end of the world, not within history, and (2) con-
cerned all the people, not just an isolated individual. In
contradistinction to this, Jesus' resurrection was both
within history and of one person...The disciples, therefore, confronted with Jesus' crucifixion and death, would
only have looked forward to the resurrection at the final
day and would probably have carefully kept their master's
tomb as a shrine, where His bones could reside until the
resurrection.[201]

In other words, the disciples' belief in the resurrection of
Christ cannot be explained as a result of either Christian belief or
Jewish teaching. There is no way to explain the origin of such a
belief apart from the fact that it happened.

This is why secular historians who study the events surrounding the origin of the church are mystified when they reject

the resurrection. The task of the historian is to adequately account for events that occur. No one doubts the church exists, but the historian cannot adequately account for it apart from Jesus still being alive. The problem for the secularist who discounts the resurrection is,

> The mysterious X is still missing. According to C.F.D. Moule of Cambridge University, here is a belief nothing in terms of previous historical influences can account for. He points out that we have a situation in which a large number of people held firmly to this belief, which cannot be explained in terms of the Old Testament or the Pharisees, and that these people held onto this belief until the Jews finally threw them out of the synagogue. According to Professor Moule, the origin of this belief must have been the fact that Jesus really did rise from the dead: "If the coming into existence of the Nazarene, a phenomenon undeniably attested by the New Testament, rips a great hole in history, a hole of the size and shape of the resurrection, what does the secular historian propose to stop it up with?…The birth and rapid rise of the Christian Church…remain an unsolved enigma for any historian who refuses to take seriously the only explanation offered by the Church itself.[202]

The resurrection of Jesus is therefore not just the best explanation; it is the *only* explanation for the origin of Christianity. Given the inability of all history to adequately explain the existence of the Christian church apart from the resurrection, how do we account for churches on every street corner of the country and throughout most of the entire planet?

Further, every book of the New Testament is based upon the conviction that Christ rose from the dead. If He never did, why were those 27 books written in the first place? And why would the apostles face the unremitting hostility and persecution of the Jewish leaders by attempting to found a new movement based on the teachings of a crucified "criminal"? Why would they continue to follow and speak about a man who was obviously a fraud or, worse, a man who made crazy predictions about His own resurrection from the dead?

On what basis would the apostles proclaim this same dead fraud—who did not resurrect—as God Himself, when their entire religious training had taught them, "Hear, O Israel, the Lord our God is one Lord"? They actually changed their beliefs from unitarianism to trinitarianism when trinitarianism was a theology never heard of before, and which for them constituted a change that was unthinkable in its magnitude. In other words, what would cause devout Jews to widely preach horrible blasphemies that went against the entire grain of their personal religious convictions and were punishable by death—except the resurrection?

Indeed, the first 20,000 or so Christians were all devout Jews, and the manner in which they changed is impossible to explain apart from the resurrection. How easily do Jews convert to Christianity today? It would have been even more difficult in the first century. All Jewish believers had five critical institutions or beliefs they held inviolate. To abandon them would be, in the words of Christian philosopher Dr. J.P. Moreland, "to risk their souls being damned to hell after death."[203] Yet all five institutions were not only abandoned or dangerously revised, they were *gladly* abandoned and dangerously revised. To our knowledge, something like this has never occurred in human history. The five institutions were:

1. the necessity to offer animal sacrifices to atone for one's sins (discarded)

2. obeying the Mosaic law for salvation and for separation from the pagan nations (discarded or revised)

3. meticulously keeping the Sabbath (dangerously revised and actually changed to celebrating "the Lord's day" on Sunday)

4. unyielding belief in monotheism (dangerously revised and changed to trinitarianism)

5. belief that the Messiah would be a political deliverer (dangerously revised to the unimaginable—an atoning Savior who was God)

Only the resurrection can explain these powerful institutions and beliefs being abandoned or drastically altered.

Just look at the facts surrounding the earliest church. A crucified Jew, despised tax collector, a hater of Jesus who killed Christians, and a few fishermen began a movement that became the largest, most influential religion on earth—an impossibility unless the resurrection really happened. Here is an obscure, unorganized movement; struggling within the loins of the ancient Roman Empire; arising within a conquered people; subject to much opposition, persecution, and suppression from the religious authorities; based entirely upon a single controversial Jew whose followers were disheartened and cynical; which somehow is able to persuade tens of thousands of skeptical Jews that this lowly carpenter, this Roman criminal tried for sedition and executed, was *their* Messiah! Even with the scandalous rumors about His birth, the allegations of insanity, the charges of His being demon-possessed—all made by the leading religious authorities of the day— tens of thousands of Jews were still persuaded that this same individual was in fact God Himself! And further, they were persuaded to quickly abandon or drastically revise virtually all of their most cherished religious institutions!

Could it ever have happened?

This unique if unstable and now even more intensely persecuted movement somehow proceeds to spread so rapidly that in just 20 years it reaches the very palace of Caesar himself in Rome (Philippians 1:13; 4:22). Not only this, it triumphs completely over scores of contending religions and ideologies and eventually overwhelms the entire Roman Empire itself—officially converting the whole kingdom to the Christian faith! If we're going to talk about historical miracles, here is one. Only a miracle can explain such a miracle.[204]

Facts are facts, and they must be explained. Again, the resurrection is not only the best explanation—it is the *only* explanation.

---

31

---

## Does the Evidence Unquestionably Convince Skeptics?

One of the most intriguing evidences for the truth of Christianity and, in particular, the resurrection of Jesus Christ is the testimony of former skeptics, many of whom set out to disprove the Christian faith.

### Saul of Tarsus

A devout Pharisee named Saul was born in Tarsus. Here he was exposed to the most advanced philosophical learning of his day. He had great command of the Greek language and considerable expertise in argument and logic. At age 14 he was sent to study under one of the greatest Jewish rabbis of the period, Gamaliel (Acts 22:3), who was probably the grandson of Hillel.

As a Hebrew zealot and Pharisee who "was advancing in Judaism beyond many Jews of my own age and was extremely zealous for the traditions of my fathers" (Galatians 1:14), Saul was not intending to disprove Christianity, but destroy it (Galatians 1:13). There is no doubt he was a skeptic both of Jesus and of the claims of Christians about the resurrection. He persecuted many Christians "to the death," and literally laid waste to the Church: "I persecuted this Way to the death, binding and putting both men and women into prisons, as also the high priest and all the Council of the elders can testify" (Acts 22:4-5; see also 8:1,3; 9:1-2,13; 22:19-20; 26:9-11 NASB).

But something changed Saul so radically the world has never quite gotten over it. Even the early Christians, after suffering such persecutions at his hand, could not believe it:

> [After his conversion] Paul immediately began to proclaim Jesus in the synagogues, saying, "He is the Son of God." And all those hearing him continued to be amazed, and were saying, "Is this not he who in Jerusalem destroyed those who called on this name, and who had come here for the purpose of bringing them bound before the chief priests?" (Acts 9:20-21).

What was it that converted the greatest enemy of the church, Saul, into its greatest defender? It was no less than a direct appearance by the risen Christ Himself—for Saul, nothing else would have sufficed. In his own words and before skeptics he recounts the experience of meeting the resurrected Christ and how it changed his life forever (Acts 26). He emphasized, "Have I not seen Jesus our Lord?" (1 Corinthians 9:1, see also Acts 22:4-21; 1 Corinthians 15:7-8).

Yet few are aware of the impact that this once-committed enemy of Christianity has had upon the world's history. Paul's three missionary journeys and lifelong evangelism and church planting helped to change the Roman Empire and even the destiny of Western civilization. Writing in *Chamber's Encyclopædia*, Archibald MacBride, professor at the University of Aberdeen, asserts of Paul, "Beside his achievements...the achievements of Alexander and Napoleon pale into insignificance."[205] Noted historian Dr. Philip Schaff emphasizes, "The conversion of Paul marks...an important epoch in the history...of mankind. It was the most fruitful event since the miracle of Pentecost, and secured the universal victory of Christianity."[206]

## Athanagoras

Athanagoras was a second-century scholar, brilliant apologist, and the first head of the eminent School of Alexandria. He originally intended to write against the faith, being "occupied with searching the Scriptures for arguments against Christianity." Instead, the evidence he discovered resulted in his conversion.[207]

## Augustine

Augustine of Hippo (354–430 A.D.) was raised in a pagan environment. At the age of 12 he was sent by his parents to the advanced schools in Madaura, a center of pagan culture and learning. He later studied and taught rhetoric in Carthage. He mastered the Latin classics, was deeply influenced by Plato, Neoplatonism, and Manicheanism, and was for a period a skeptic of religion. But after careful reading of the Bible and hearing the sermons of Bishop Ambrose while in Milan, he was converted to the Christian faith and became the greatest Father of the Western church. His two most famous works are *Confessions* and the *City of God*, but he also wrote apologetic texts such as *Contra Academicos* (Against the Academics), a critique of the academic skeptics of his day.[208]

The next 14 centuries contain thousands of additional testimonies of converted skeptics.

## George Lyttleton and Gilbert West

In the mid-eighteenth century Lord George Lyttleton (a member of Parliament and Commissioner of the Treasury) and Gilbert West went to Oxford. There they were determined to attack the very basis of Christianity. Lyttleton set out to prove that Saul of Tarsus was never converted to Christianity, and West intended to demonstrate that Jesus never rose from the dead. Each planned to do a painstaking job, taking a full year to establish their case. But as they proceeded, they eventually concluded that Christianity was true. Both became Christians. West eventually wrote *Observations on the History and Evidences of the Resurrection of Jesus Christ* (1747). George Lyttleton wrote a lengthy text titled *The Conversion of St. Paul* (1749). Their correspondence back and forth, showing their surprise at the quality of the evidence, can be found in any university microfilm library. West was totally convinced of the resurrection and Lyttleton of the conversion of Paul on the basis of it. For example, Lyttleton wrote to West in 1761,

Sir, in a late conversation we had together upon the subject of the Christian religion, I told you that besides all the proofs of it which may be drawn from the prophecies of the Old Testament, from the necessary connection it has with the whole system of the Jewish religion, from the miracles of Christ, and from the evidence given of his reflection by all the other apostles, I thought the conversion and apostleship of Saint Paul alone, duly considered, was of itself a demonstration sufficient to prove Christianity a divine revelation.[209]

## Frank Morison

In the twentieth century, the conversion of skeptics and doubters has continued. In the 1930s a rationalistic English journalist named Frank Morison attempted to discover the "real" Jesus Christ. He was convinced that Christ's "history rested upon very insecure foundations," largely because of the influence of the rationalistic higher criticism so prevalent in his day.[210] Further, he was dogmatically opposed to the miraculous elements in the Gospels. But he was nevertheless fascinated by the person of Jesus, who was to him "an almost legendary figure of purity and noble manhood."[211] Morison decided to take the crucial "last phase" in the life of Christ and

> to strip it of its overgrowth of primitive beliefs and dogmatic suppositions, and to see this supremely great Person as he really was...It seemed to me that if I could come at the truth why this man died a cruel death at the hands of the Roman Power, how he himself regarded the matter, and especially how he behaved under the test, I should be very near to the true solution of the problem.[212]

But the book that Morison ended up writing was not the one he intended to. He came to see the truth of the Gospels and proceeded to write one of the most able defenses of the resurrection of Christ in our time, *Who Moved the Stone?*

## Cyril Joad

Dr. Cyril E.M. Joad, head of the Philosophy Department at the University of London, once believed that Jesus was only a man. For many years, he was an antagonist toward Christianity. But near the end of his life he came to believe that the only solution for mankind was "found in the cross of Jesus Christ." He became a zealous disciple.[213]

## Giovanni Papine

Giovanni Papine was one of the foremost Italian intellects of his period, an atheist, a vocal enemy of the church, and a self-appointed debunker of religion. But he became converted to faith in Christ and in 1921 penned his *Life of Christ*, stunning most of his friends and admirers.[214]

## C. S. Lewis

The Cambridge and Oxford scholar C.S. Lewis, a former atheist, was converted to Christianity on the basis of the evidence, according to his text *Surprised by Joy*. He recalls, "I thought I had the Christians 'placed' and disposed of forever." But, "A young man who wishes to remain a sound atheist cannot be too careful of his reading. There are traps everywhere—'Bibles laid open, millions of surprises,' as Herbert says, 'Fine nets and stratagems.' God is, if I may say it, very unscrupulous."[215] C.S. Lewis became a Christian because the evidence was compelling and he could not escape it. Even against his will he was "brought in kicking, struggling, resentful, and darting [my] eyes in every direction for a chance of escape." The God "whom I so earnestly desired not to meet" became his Lord and Savior.[216] His book on Christian evidences, *Mere Christianity*, is considered a classic and has been responsible for converting thousands to the faith, among them the keen legal mind of former skeptic and Watergate figure Charles Colson, author of quality books such as *Born Again, Burden of Truth: Defending the Truth in an Age of Unbelief*, and *Loving God*.

## Josh McDowell

As a pre-law student, Josh McDowell was also a skeptic of Christianity and believed that every Christian had two minds: One was lost and the other was out looking for it. Eventually challenged to intellectually investigate Christian truth claims and thinking it a farce, he accepted the challenge—"as a result, I found historical facts and evidence about Jesus Christ that I never knew existed."[217] He eventually wrote a number of important texts in defense of Christianity, among them *Evidence That Demands a Verdict, More Evidence That Demands a Verdict* (a detailed critique of higher critical theories), *More Than a Carpenter*, and *Daniel in the Lion's Den.*

## Gary Habermas

Dr. Gary Habermas has two doctorates and has written over 100 articles and 22 books (nine on Jesus' resurrection, including *The Resurrection of Jesus: A Rational Inquiry, The Resurrection of Jesus: An Apologetic,* and *Did Jesus Rise from the Dead?: The Resurrection Debate,* plus other apologetic works such as *Dealing With Doubt*). He was President of the Evangelical Philosophical Society, and has debated leading atheists. Raised in a Christian home, he began to question his faith. He concluded that while the resurrection might be believed, he personally doubted it and was skeptical that any evidence for it was actually convincing. After critical examination, it was the evidence that brought him to the conclusion that the resurrection was an established fact of history.[218]

## John Warwick Montgomery

As a brilliant philosophy student at Cornell University, Montgomery was a convinced skeptic when it came to Christianity. But he, too, was challenged to investigate the evidence for Christianity. As a result, he became converted. He recalls, "I went to university as a 'garden-variety' twentieth-century pagan. And as a result of being forced, for intellectual integrity's sake, to check out this evidence, I finally came around."[219] He confessed that had it not been for a committed undergraduate student who continued to challenge him to really examine the evidence, he would never have believed: "I thank God that he cared enough to do the reading to become a good apologist because if I hadn't had someone like that I don't know if I would have become a Christian."[220] Montgomery went on to graduate from Cornell University with distinction in philosophy, Phi Beta Kappa. Then he earned his Ph.D. from the University of Chicago, a second doctorate in theology from the University of Strasbourg, France, and seven additional graduate degrees in theology, law, library science, and other fields. He has served on the faculty of the University of Chicago and was Chairman of the Department of History at Wilfrid Laurier University, Canada. He is internationally regarded both as a theologian and as a lawyer (barrister-at-law of the Middle Temple and Lincoln's Inn, England; member of the California, Virginia, Washington State, and District of Columbia Bars and the Bar of the Supreme Court of the United States). He is one of only six persons to have received the Diploma of the International Institute of Human Rights cum laude, and was the Institute's Director of Studies from 1979 to 1981. He has written more than 130 scholarly journal articles and over 40 books, many of them defending the Christian faith against skeptical views. He has held numerous prestigious appointments, is a founding member of the World Association of Law Professors, a member of the American Society of International Law, and is honored in *Who's Who in America, Who's Who in American Law, The Directory of American Scholars, International Scholars Directory, Who's Who in France, Who's Who in Europe,* and *Who's Who in the World.*

## Malcolm Muggeridge

Among great literary writers, few can match the famed author Malcolm Muggeridge. He too was once a skeptic of Christianity, but near the end of his life became fully convinced of the truth of the resurrection of Christ, writing a book acclaimed by critics,

*Jesus: The Man Who Lives*. In it, Muggeridge wrote, "The coming of Jesus into the world is the most stupendous event in human history," and "What is unique about Jesus is that, on the testimony and in the experience of innumerable people, of all sorts and conditions, of all races and nationalities from the simplest and most primitive to the most sophisticated and cultivated, he remains alive." Muggeridge concludes, "That the resurrection happened... seems to me indubitably true" and "either Jesus never was or he still is...with the utmost certainty, I assert he still is."[221]

## Sir William M. Ramsay

Sir William M. Ramsay was a classical scholar, archaeologist (he became the first Professor of Classical Art and Archaeology at Oxford), and the foremost authority of his day on the topography, antiquities, and history of Asia Minor in ancient times. He was educated at Oxford, becoming a professor at both Oxford and Cambridge. He received many academic distinctions: the gold medal of Pope Leo XIII, the Victoria medal of the Royal Geographical Society, and gold medals from the University of Pennsylvania and the Royal Scottish Geographical Society. He was knighted in 1906 on the four hundredth anniversary of the University of Aberdeen for distinguished service to the scholarly world. He was recipient of three honorary fellowships from Oxford colleges (Exeter in 1898, Lincoln in 1899, and St. John's in 1912), and was honored with doctorates from nine universities: Oxford, St. Andrews, Glasgow, Aberdeen, Cambridge, Edinburgh, New York, Bordeaux, and Marburg. He was also an original member of the British Academy "and an honorary member of just about every scholarly association devoted to archaeological and historical research." This biographer notes that

> He always insisted upon originality in research and first-hand acquaintance with the facts...Two things characterize Ramsay above all else. He was original and he was thorough. He writes this in the introduction to his *Historical Geography*: "My scheme has been (after several experiences

of the difficulties caused by accepting wrong conjectures of modern writers) to make an absolutely fresh work founded on the ancient authorities alone, in which the geographical situation, the natural surroundings and the commercial advantages of each city should be set forth in an account of its history." Ninety-five per cent of the references made to ancient writers in his work, the reader is assured, were found by the author in his own perusal of the original authorities, most of whom were read several times in the original. This is quite a feat, for he quotes from 90 different ancient writers, from classical historians to early church fathers, in both Greek and Latin.[222]

But Ramsay was also a skeptic of Christianity, convinced the Bible was fraudulent. He spent years preparing himself for the announced task of heading an expedition into Asia Minor and Palestine, to "dig up the evidence" that the Bible was a fraud. After 15 years of digging, he published a large volume on *St. Paul the Roman Citizen and Traveler.*

The book caused a furor of dismay among the skeptics of the world. Its attitude was utterly unexpected, because it was contrary to the announced intention of the author years before…for 20 years more, book after book from the same author came from the press, each filled with additional evidence of the exact, minute truthfulness of the whole New Testament as tested by the spade on the spot. The evidence was so overwhelming that many infidels announced their repudiation of their former unbelief and accepted Christianity. And these books have stood the test of time, not one having been refuted, nor have I found even any attempt to refute them.[223]

Ramsay's own exhaustive archaeological work and findings convinced him of the reliability of the Bible and the truth of what it taught, as seen in *The Bearing of Recent Discovery on the Trustworthiness of the New Testament; The Church in the Roman Empire before A.D. 170; Luke the Physician; The First Christian Century,* and others. For example, "Without a single error, Luke was accurate in naming 32 countries, 54 cities, and 9 islands..." Ramsay finally had this to say: "I began with a mind unfavorable to it...but more recently I found myself brought into contact with the Book of Acts as an authority for the topography, antiquities, and society of Asia Minor. It was gradually borne upon me that in various details the narrative showed marvelous truth."[224]

## John Scott

Dr. Scott was of the greatest classical scholars of the twentieth century, an outstanding authority on Homer. He was also a president of the American Philosophical Association and president of the Classical Association of the Midwest and South. For 40 years he was professor of Greek at Northwestern University. At age 70 he wrote a book concluding a lifetime of ripened convictions: *We Would See Jesus*. He, too, became convinced that Luke was an accurate historian: "Luke was not only a doctor and historian, but he was one of the world's greatest men of letters. He wrote the clearest and the best Greek written in that century."[225]

## Lee Strobel

Lee Strobel was an award-winning reporter for the *Chicago Tribune*, with an M.S. in Law from Yale. He was also a convinced skeptic and atheist.

> For much of my life I was a skeptic. In fact, I considered myself an atheist...I had read just enough philosophy and history to find support for my skepticism...I had a strong motivation to ignore [any problems with skepticism]: a self-serving and immoral lifestyle that I would be compelled to abandon if I were ever to change my views and become a follower of Jesus. As far as I was concerned, the case was closed.

When his beloved wife Leslie announced the news she had become a Christian, he was stunned:

I rolled my eyes and braced for the worst, feeling like the victim of a bait-and-switch scam. I had married one Leslie—the fun Leslie, the carefree Leslie, the risk-taking Leslie—and now I feared she was going to turn into some sort of sexually repressed prude who would trade our upwardly mobile lifestyle for all-night prayer vigils and volunteer work in grimy soup kitchens. Instead I was pleasantly surprised—even fascinated—by the fundamental changes in her character, her integrity, and her personal confidence. Eventually I wanted to get to the bottom of what was prompting the subtle but significant shifts in my wife's attitudes, so I launched an all-out investigation into the facts surrounding the case for Christianity.

A two-year investigation was undertaken with a hard-nosed reporter's skepticism, training in law, and lots of study:

> Setting aside my self-interest and prejudices as best I could, I read books, interviewed experts, asked questions, analyzed history, explored archaeology, studied ancient literature, and for the first time in my life picked apart the Bible verse by verse...I applied the training I had received at Yale Law School as well as my experience as legal affairs editor of the *Chicago Tribune*. And over time the evidence of the world—of history, of science, of philosophy, of psychology—began to point toward the unthinkable.

After a two-year investigation he found he had to bow before the evidence and concluded:

> I'll admit it: I was ambushed by the amount and quality of the evidence that Jesus is the unique son of God. As I sat at my desk that Sunday afternoon, I shook my head in amazement. I see defendants carted off to the death chamber on much less convincing proof! The cumulative facts and data all pointed unmistakably toward a conclusion that I wasn't entirely comfortable in reaching ...It would require much more faith for me to maintain my atheism than to trust in Jesus of Nazareth!... in fact, my mind could not conjure up a single explanation that fit the evidence of history nearly as

well as the conclusion that Jesus was the one he claimed to be: the one and only Son of God…After a personal investigation that spanned more than 600 days and countless hours, my own verdict in the case for Christ was clear…The case for Christ is conclusive.

Indeed, even from the mouths of babes: "A few months after I became a follower of Jesus, our five-year-old daughter Allison went up to my wife and said, 'Mommy, I want God to do for me what he's done for Daddy.'"[226] Strobel's books, *The Case for Christ: A Journalist's Personal Investigation of the Evidence for Jesus, The Case for Faith: A Journalist Investigates the Toughest Objections to Christianity, God's Outrageous Claims,* and *Inside the Mind of Unchurched Harry and Mary,* are valuable for the inquiring or skeptical mind.

### Guy Cramer

Ion scientist and geophysicist Guy Cramer recalls, "I can relate with Saul/Paul, as I was the atheist of atheists. Anything Christian created an emotional swelling of hatred. I could argue with the best. I never argued other religions (they never created any emotional response), just Christianity…[But] I eventually read enough compelling evidence that I came to faith that Jesus was the son of God." He went on to develop the intriguing 'YFiles' site which contains files on many of the questions he had about Christianity as a skeptic.[227]

### Mike Licona

As a Christian, Mike Licona began to wonder if Christianity was true after all. After detailed study, he published *Cross Examined.* Set in a courtroom drama, it centers around a trial that presents an evidential cross examination and defense of the resurrection. He also wrote the legal brief used for a National Clergy Council "moot court" held in Washington, D.C. on April 6, 2001 on "The Evidence for the Resurrection of Jesus Christ."[228]

Such testimonies could be multiplied indefinitely. Books such as *Philosophers Who Believe* and *The Intellectuals Speak Out About God: A Handbook for the Christian Student in a Secular Society* can be found in many disciplines and show that the process of conversion continues and will continue until His return.

What is interesting is that we do not find such testimonies like this—of skeptics converting to religious faith on the basis of independently confirmed evidence—in any other religion. If truth is its own testimony, Christianity must be true.

## 32

### WOULD THE EVIDENCE OF THE RESURRECTION STAND CROSS-EXAMINATION IN A MODERN LAW COURT?

Keep in mind what is being claimed here. After all the evidence is presented, the truth of an astonishing miracle would actually be confirmed and bring in a positive verdict from a modern law court. In other words, the most incredible miracle, one of tremendous import for every human being, will stand the best evidential rebuttal that plaintiff attorneys can muster. The most significant event to all people everywhere will survive critical cross-examination in a modern court of law. Is there any other religion that can make such a claim?

In Acts 1:3, the physician Luke tells us that Jesus Christ "presented Himself alive after His suffering by many infallible proofs" (NASB). The Greek *en pollois tekmariois* is an expression which is defined in the lexicons as "decisive proof" "and indicates the strongest type of legal evidence.[229] Lawyers are expertly trained to deal with evidence in all areas. As Strobel noted in his own search, "In this quest for truth, I've used my experience as legal affairs journalist to look at numerous categories of proof—eyewitness evidence, documentary evidence, corroborating evidence, rebuttal evidence, scientific evidence, psychological evidence, circumstantial evidence, and, yes, even fingerprint evidence."[230]

Skeptics can, if they wish, maintain that only the weak-minded would believe in the literal, physical resurrection of Christ, but perhaps this only reveals their own weak-mindedness when it comes to taking the evidence at face value. To establish their counterclaims, skeptics (or higher critics that run theological lotteries like the so-called "Jesus Seminar") have to provide real evidence in support of their beliefs, not just conjecture, biased opinions, or foolishness. One can only wonder why it is that in 2000 years some of the best minds humanity can muster have never been able to prove their skeptical theories, or offer a convincing defense of them.

Lawyers aren't the weak-minded. Lawyers are expertly trained in the matter of evaluating evidence and are perhaps the most qualified in the task of weighing data critically. Is it coincidence that so many of them throughout history have concluded in favor of the truth of the Christian religion? Hundreds of lawyers are represented by The National Christian Legal Society, The O.W. Coburn School of Law, The Rutherford Institute, Lawyers Christian Fellowship, Simon Greenleaf University/Trinity Law School, Regent University School of Law, and other Christian law organizations, schools, and societies. Among their number are some of the most respected lawyers in the country, people who have graduated from our leading law schools and gone on to prominence in the world of law. The law schools of Cornell, Harvard, Yale, Boston, New York University, University of Southern California, Georgetown, University of Michigan, Northwestern, Hastings College of Law at U.C. Berkeley, Loyola, and many others are all represented in these organizations.

As to the evidence for the resurrection of Christ, consider the testimony of some of the finest lawyers in history and today. We have cited Christian lawyers simply because non-Christian lawyers had not examined the evidence or weren't interested in examining it. Christian lawyers were the only ones familiar with the evidence, but the ones we cite are highly qualified, and many were former skeptics. Nevertheless, we would hope that unbelieving or skeptical lawyers would also devise their own "moot court."

Lord Darling, a former lord chief justice in England, asserts, "In its favor as a living truth there exists such overwhelming evidence, positive and negative, factual and circumstantial, that no intelligent jury in the world could fail to bring in a verdict that the resurrection story is true."[231]

John Singleton Copley (Lord Lyndhurst, 1772–1863) is recognized as one of the greatest legal minds in British history. He was solicitor general of the British government, attorney general of Great Britain, three times the high chancellor of England, and elected high steward of the University of Cambridge. He challenges, "I know pretty well what evidence is; and I tell you, such evidence as that for the resurrection has never broken down yet."[232]

Hugo Grotius (1583–1645) was a noted "jurist and scholar whose works are of fundamental importance in international law," according to the *Encyclopaedia Britannica*. He mastered Latin by the age of eight, entered Leiden University at 11, and took his doctorate at 15. King Henry IV was so impressed by him he pronounced him "The Miracle of Holland." Taking a law degree in France, he then came home at 16 to publish a revision of Capella's encyclopedia so influential that a critical edition was published in Leipzig in 1866. At 24 he was appointed Attorney General for Holland, Zeeland, and West-Friesland. Considered "the father of international law," he wrote *The Truth of the Christian Religion* (1622, 1971), a debating manual for European sailors to help them convert others, in which he defended the historic fact of the resurrection.[233] It was published in 13 languages, including Arabic and Urdu. In England the Latin version was actually a standard school text up through the mid-1800s. Grotius' conclusion was that many people *had* seen Jesus, and

> it would have been impossible for so many to conspire together to perpetrate such a hoax...There is not, neither ever was there any other Religion in the whole world, that

can be imagined more honourable for excellency of reward, more absolute and perfect for precepts, or more admirable for the manner according to which it was commanded to be propagated and divulged.[234]

J.N.D. Anderson, in the words of Armand Nicholi of the Harvard Medical School (*Christianity Today*, March 29, 1968), is a scholar of international repute eminently qualified to deal with the subject of evidence. He is one of the world's leading authorities on Muslim law, Dean of the Faculty of Law at the University of London, chairman of the Department of Oriental Law at the School of Oriental and African Studies, and director of the Institute of Advanced Legal Studies at the University of London.[235] In Anderson's text, *Christianity: The Witness of History*, he supplies the standard evidences for the resurrection and asks, "How, then, can the fact of the resurrection be denied?"[236] Anderson further emphasizes, "Lastly, it can be asserted with confidence that men and women disbelieve the Easter story not because of the evidence but in spite of it."[237]

Sir Edward Clark observes,

> As a lawyer, I have made a prolonged study of the evidences for the events of the first Easter day. To me the evidence is conclusive, and over and over again in the High Court I have secured the verdict on evidence not nearly so compelling. Inference follows on evidence, and a truthful witness is always artless and disdains effect. The gospel evidence for the resurrection is of this class, and as a lawyer I accept it unreservedly as a testimony of truthful men to facts they were able to substantiate.[238]

Irwin H. Linton was a Washington, D.C. lawyer who argued cases before the U.S. Supreme Court. In *A Lawyer Examines the Bible*, he challenges his fellow lawyers "by every acid test known to the law...to examine the case for the Bible just as they would any important matter submitted to their professional attention by a client." He believes that the evidence for Christianity is "overwhelming" and that at least "three independent and converging lines of proof," each of which "is conclusive in itself," establish the truth of the Christian faith. Linton observed that "the logical, historical...proofs of...Christianity are so indisputable that I have found them to arrest the surprised attention of just about every man to whom I have presented them." He further argues the resurrection "is not only so established that the greatest lawyers have declared it to be the best proved fact of all history, but it is so supported that it is difficult to conceive of any method or line of proof that it lacks which would make [it] more certain."

He concluded the claims of Christian faith are so well established by such a variety of independent and converging proofs that "it has been said again and again by great lawyers that they cannot but be regarded as proved under the strictest rules of evidence used in the highest American and English courts."[239]

Simon Greenleaf was the Royal Professor of Law at Harvard and author of the classic three-volume text, *A Treatise on the Law of Evidence* (1842), which, according to Dr. Wilbur Smith, "is still considered the greatest single authority on evidence in the entire literature on legal procedure."[240] Greenleaf himself is considered one of the greatest authorities on common-law evidence in Western history. The *London Law Journal* wrote of him in 1874, "It is no mean honor to America that her schools of jurisprudence have produced two of the finest writers and best esteemed legal authorities in this century—the great and good man, Judge Story, and his eminent and worthy associate Professor Greenleaf. Upon the existing law of evidence (by Greenleaf) more light has shown from the New World than from all the lawyers who adorn the courts of Europe."[241] H.W.H. Knotts in the *Dictionary of American Biography* says of him, "To the efforts of Story and Greenleaf is ascribed the rise of the Harvard Law School to its eminent position among the legal schools of the United States." Greenleaf concluded that the resurrection of Christ was one of the best supported events in history, according to the laws of legal evidence administered in courts of justice.[242] He writes,

All that Christianity asks of men…is, that they would be consistent with themselves; that they would treat its evidences as they treat the evidence of other things; and that they would try and judge its actors and witnesses, as they deal with their fellow men, when testifying to human affairs and actions, in human tribunals. Let the witnesses [to the resurrection] be compared with themselves, with each other, and with surrounding facts and circumstances; and let their testimony be sifted, as if it were given in a court of justice, on the side of the adverse party, the witness being subjected to a rigorous cross-examination. The result, it is confidently believed, will be an undoubting conviction of their integrity, ability and truth.[243]

Lord Caldecote, lord chief justice of England, observed that an "overwhelming case for the resurrection could be made merely as a matter of strict evidence."[244]

Thomas Sherlock's *Trial of the Witnesses of the Resurrection of Jesus Christ* places the resurrection in a legally argued forum and in the words of lawyer Irwin Linton, "will give anyone so reading it the comfortable assurance that he knows the utmost that can be said against the proof of the central fact of our faith and also how utterly every such attack can be met and answered."[245]

The above sample citations show that we have some 400 years of legal testimony as to the validity of the resurrection, according to the standards of legal evidence, confirming St. Luke's specific use of words in Acts 1:3. In what other religion is anything even remotely comparable? Although admissibility rules vary by state and no lawyer can guarantee the decision of any jury (no matter how persuasive the evidence), an abundance of lawyers will testify today that the resurrection would stand in the vast majority of law courts. The following statements were received in written form from the individuals cited as a result of phone conversations held on March 26–28, 1990, January 10, 1995, or in January 2002.

John Whitehead is founder of the Rutherford Institute and one of the leading constitutional attorneys in America. He asserts,

"The evidence for the resurrection, if competently presented, would likely be affirmed in a modern law court."

Larry Donahue is an experienced trial attorney in Los Angeles. He has 20 years' experience with courtroom law trials. He also teaches courses on legal evidence at Simon Greenleaf University in Anaheim, California, (now a division of Trinity Law School of Trinity International University, Deerfield, Illinois) as well as a lengthy course subjecting the biblical eyewitnesses to legal cross examination titled, "The Resurrection on Trial." He states: "I am convinced that in a civil lawsuit in nearly any courtroom today there is more than sufficient admissible direct and circumstantial evidence that a jury could be persuaded to a preponderance burden of proof that the physical bodily resurrection of Christ did occur."

Richard F. Duncan holds a national reputation as a legal scholar whose area of specialty is constitutional law. He graduated from Cornell Law School (where he wrote for the *Law Review*) and practiced corporate law at White and Case, a major Wall Street law firm. He has spent 11 years teaching at such law schools as Notre Dame and New York University and is a tenured professor at the University of Nebraska. Mr. Duncan has written briefs at the Supreme Court level and is the author of a standard text on commercial law widely used by attorneys practicing under the Uniform Commercial Code, *The Law in Practice of Secure Transaction*. He observes, "The resurrection of Jesus Christ, the central fact of world history, withstands rational analysis precisely because the evidence is so persuasive...I am convinced this verdict would stand in nearly any modern court of law."

A. Eric Johnston is currently a member of the law firm of Seier, Johnston, and Trippe in Birmingham, Alabama. He practices in the areas of constitutional law, federal statutory law, and litigation in the federal and state courts on the trial and appellate levels. He is a member of the American Bar Association, was the 1988 Republican nominee for place four on the Alabama Supreme Court, and has been listed as one of the Outstanding Young Men of America and in *Who's Who in American Law*. He states, "In a civil court, if the evidence were properly presented, I believe this would be sufficient for a jury to find that Christ did rise from the dead."

Donovan Campbell, Jr., is a graduate of Princeton University and the University of Texas, where he was editor of the *Texas Law Review*. He was admitted to the Texas Bar in 1975; the U.S. Tax Court in 1976; the U.S. Court of Claims in 1977; and the U.S. Court of Appeals for the Fifth Circuit in 1978. He has had wide experience in the field of law and litigation. He states, "If the evidence for the resurrection were competently presented to a normal jury in a civil court of law at the current time, then a verdict establishing the fact of the resurrection should be obtained."

Wendell R. Byrd is an Atlanta attorney and graduate of Yale Law School. As a student, he was the first ever to exempt the freshman year at Vanderbilt University, where he graduated summa cum laude; he also received Yale's prize for one of the best two student publications. He is a member of the most prestigious legal organization, The American Law Institute, has published in the *Yale Law Journal, Harvard Journal of Law,* and *Public Policy,* and has argued before the U.S. Supreme Court. He is listed in *Who's Who in the World, Who's Who in the South and Southwest,* and *Who's Who Among Emerging Leaders in America.* He asserts: "In a civil trial I believe the evidence is sufficient that a modern jury should bring in a positive verdict that the resurrection of Christ did happen."

William Burns Lawless is a retired justice of the New York Supreme Court and former dean of Notre Dame Law School. He asserts, "When Professor Simon Greenleaf of Harvard Law School published his distinguished treatise on the Law of Evidence in 1842, he analyzed the resurrection accounts in the Gospels. Under the rules of evidence then he concluded a Court would admit these accounts and consider their contents reliable. In my opinion that conclusion is as valid in 1995 as it was in 1842."

In *Leading Lawyers Look at the Resurrection,* many other examples are given. For example: Sir Lionell Luckhoo is listed in the *Guinness Book of Records* as the world's "most successful lawyer," with 245 successive murder acquittals. He was knighted twice by the queen of England and appointed high commissioner for Guyana. He declares, "I have spent more than 42 years as a defense trial lawyer appearing in many parts of the world...I say unequivocally the evidence for the resurrection of Jesus Christ is so overwhelming that it compels acceptance by proof which leaves absolutely no doubt."[246]

Dale Foreman, a graduate of the Harvard Law School and lawyer in Washington state, writes in *Crucify Him: A Lawyer Looks at the Trial of Jesus,*

> These facts [the trial, crucifixion, and death of Christ], I believe, are clear and proven beyond a reasonable doubt...The teachings of Jesus have changed the world. In 2000 years not a day has gone by when the influence of this itinerate teacher from Nazareth has not been felt. As a trial lawyer, I am trained to be rational, skeptical, and critical. I believe it improbable that any fraud or false Messiah could have made such a profound impression for good. The most reasonable conclusion, and the most satisfying, is that Jesus was indeed the Son of God, that He was who He claimed to be, and that He did come back to life.[247]

Francis Lamb, a Wisconsin lawyer, is the author of *Miracle and Science*, which tests the credibility of biblical miracles through legal examination. He asserts, "Tested by the standards or ordeals of jural science by which questions of fact are ascertained and demonstrated in the contested questions of right between man and man in courts of justice, the resurrection of Jesus stands as a demonstrated fact."[248]

In addition, we may refer to Sir Leslie Herron, chief justice of New South Wales, Australia; Frank J. Powell, the outstanding English magistrate and author of the scholarly *The Trial of Jesus Christ*; and also Mr. Clarrie Briese, a distinguished Australian lawyer, awarded a Churchill Fellowship, graduate of Cambridge University, and chief magistrate of New South Wales and author of *Witnesses to the Resurrection—Credible or Not?*[249] But such citations could be multiplied on and on. We have not mentioned the eminent Lord Chancellor Hailsham, the current lord chancellor of England and Wales,[250] Lord Diplock,[251] or Joseph J. Darlington, the only lawyer in the nation's capital to whom a public monument has been erected, and who former president and chief justice of the U.S. Supreme Court William Howard Taft said was one of the three or four greatest lawyers in the nation's history.[252] We have not mentioned Sir Matthew Hale (the great lord chancellor under Oliver Cromwell), John Seldon, Sir Robert Anderson (former head of Scotland Yard and knighted by Queen Victoria for his utmost skill in exposing "the mazes of falsehood ...discovering truth and separating it from error"), Daniel Webster, Lord Erskine, or many others.[253]

But it is not merely in the field of law that we find committed believers in Christ's resurrection. For example, societies of Christian believers exist for most scholarly disciplines, including philosophy, history, mathematics, medicine, literature, education, biology, nursing, economics, pharmacy, engineering, psychology, and sociology.[254] Collectively they include thousands of members among whom are some of the most erudite minds of our time. Yet all of them believe in the physical resurrection of Christ because they find the evidence convincing. For example, among philosophers we could cite Basil Mitchell, for many years the Nolloth Professor of the Christian Religion at Oxford University and author of *The Justification of Religious Belief*. Alvin Plantinga of Notre Dame has taught at Yale, Harvard, UCLA, Boston University, and University of Chicago, and has been president of the American Philosophical Association and the Society of Christian Philosophers. He is the author of *God and Other Minds: A Study of the Rational Justification of Belief in God* which the *Journal of Philosophy* called "one of the most important" books on the philosophy of religion in the twentieth century. Richard Swineburn of Oxford University is widely known as one of the premier rational defenders of Christian faith in the twentieth century and is author of *The Christian God* and *The Coherence of Theism, Faith and Reason.* Mortimer J. Adler has held professorships at Columbia University and the University of Chicago, is director of the Institute for Philosophical Research, chairman of the board of editors of the *Encyclopædia Britannica,* architect of The Great Books of the Western World and its *Syntopicon,* and author of more than 50 books including *Truth in Religion, Ten Philosophical Mistakes,* and *How to Think About God.* [255]

Hundreds of other distinguished names could also be added from other scholarly disciplines. The point is this: The quality and quantity of the evidence for the resurrection and Christianity is matched by the quality and quantity of the testimony to its legitimacy. We have shown that both those who were committed skeptics and those who are expertly trained to sift evidence have declared that the resurrection of Jesus Christ is a historic fact.

---

### 33

## HOW CREDIBLE ARE THE ALTERNATE THEORIES PROPOSED OVER 2000 YEARS?

But that doesn't mean our job is quite over. Historically, critics have proposed a number of theories to explain the resurrection on other grounds, and these must at least be briefly addressed. These theories do not decrease our faith in the resurrection. They increase it by showing they are empty ideas which explain nothing, and that only the Christian explanation is true. Ever since the time of Jesus (Matthew 28:11-15), critics have been attempting to explain the empty tomb on naturalistic grounds. Indeed, in 2000 years many different theories have been proposed, but "not one of these theories has ever met with general acceptance, even among radical critics and rationalists."[256] This includes the following "grasping at straws" theories, all of which have been entirely refuted, most for centuries: the swoon theory, "Passover Plot" or conspiracy theory, stolen or moved body theory, hallucination/

vision theory, telegram/telegraph theory, mistaken identity theory, wrong tomb/grave was not visited theory, séance theory, annihilation theory, Jesus never existed and resurrection as legend theory, resurrection as mystery religion theory, and others.

Anyone who takes the time to carefully compare these theories to the four Gospel resurrection accounts quickly discovers that they are highly inferior explanations, grossly conflicting at many points with each other and, more importantly, with the biblical evidence itself. The fundamental problem for the critic is that he has yet to propose *any* theory that reasonably accounts for all the historical data to the satisfaction of believer and skeptic alike. For example, consider that even biblical critics admit that the earliest Christian hymns and creeds, such as Philippians 2:6-11 and 1 Corinthians 15:3-8, give key facts about the death and resurrection of Christ, including a detailed list of those he appeared to. But according to a leading authority on the historicity of the Gospels, Dr. Craig Blomberg, these can "be dated to within two years of that very event."[257] Legends cannot develop in two years— that would constitute a much greater miracle than the resurrection. The time necessary for legends to be generated would take us into the second century, which, in fact, is exactly when the legendary apocryphal Gospels begin to appear. "When German theologian Julius Muller in 1844 challenged anyone to find a single example of legend developing that fast anywhere in history, the response from the scholars of his day—and to the present time— was resounding silence."[258]

Indeed, modern skeptics face the same problems that skeptics at the time of Jesus faced: the empty tomb and the resurrection appearances. No one could disprove the empty tomb or explain away the resurrection appearances then, and no one can do so today. As noted scholar Wilbur Smith asserts, "The closest, most critical examination of these narratives throughout the ages never has destroyed and never can destroy their powerful testimony to the truth that Christ did rise from the dead on the third day, and was seen by many."[259] Both the empty grave and the resurrection appearances provide "a mass of evidence that can never be destroyed with any of the laws of literary criticism or of logic known to man. They have, consequently, stood the fiercest opposition, investigation, and criticism of at least 18 successive centuries."[260]

It is difficult to know which is the more amazing thing: the alternate theories themselves or the fact that they continue to be put forth by otherwise intelligent men. These theories are not only improbable; they are, in the end, impossible. There is no literary or historical evidence for their support, and the historical facts refute them all. The final deathblow to these theories is that each of them refutes something of the others until nothing is left. In other words, theory A, in proposing sub-theory B, discredits theory C, and so on. They all collapse for the simple reason that although each critical theory rejects part of the Gospel testimony, each also accepts and independently establishes the truth of another part of the Gospel testimony. Taken together, all the critical theories of the nineteenth and twentieth centuries establish both the reliability of the New Testament as well as the unreliability of the alternate critical theories. As Dr. Gary Habermas observes,

> One interesting illustration of this failure of the naturalistic theories is that they were disproved by the nineteenth-century older liberals themselves, [the very ones] by whom these theories were popularized. These scholars refuted each other's theories, leaving no viable naturalistic hypotheses…Although nineteenth-century liberals decimated each other's views individually, twentieth-century critical scholars have generally rejected naturalistic theories as a whole, judging that they are incapable of explaining the known data…That even such critical scholars have rejected these naturalistic theories is a significant epitaph for the failure of these views.[261]

In conclusion, since the time of Christ, no attempt to offer credible evidence against the bodily resurrection of Christ has succeeded. This in itself is extremely significant. Consider just a few conclusions of scholars who have studied these theories. James Orr: "None of these theories can stand calm examination...."[262] George Hanson: "The simple faith of the Christian who believes in the resurrection is nothing compared to the credulity of the skeptic who will accept the wildest and most improbable romances rather than admit the plain witness of historical certainties."[263] Wilbur M. Smith: "Of the several attempts to explain rationalistically the empty tomb...it need only be said that none is inherently credible or has commanded general respect."[264] John Warwick Montgomery: "they are infinitely more improbable than the resurrection itself, and they fly squarely in the face of the documentary evidence."[265] John Lilly: "The field of biblical criticism resembles a vast graveyard filled with the skeletons of discarded theories devised by highly imaginative skeptics...One might think that so many repeated failures...would lead the opposition to abandon their efforts, but not so. They continue unabated, and men are still wracking their brains, working their imaginations overtime, and parading a vast amount of erudition and ingenuity in their, to us, futile attempts to destroy the impregnable rock of historical evidence on which the Christian faith in the resurrection stands proud and unshaken."[266] Sir Norman Anderson: "the empty tomb, then, forms a veritable rock on which all rationalistic theories of the resurrection dash themselves in vain."[267]

In the end, facts will always win because facts, unlike conjecture, cannot be changed or disproved. To pursue extraordinary, even desperate theories against clear historical evidence is not being scholarly, but silly.

---

## 34

# WHAT HAPPENS TO THE EVIDENCE IN SCHOLARLY DEBATE?

Our final evidence for the resurrection will be to show that it stands tall in the arena of scholarly debate forums. In the last two decades, more than a thousand debate forums have been held between skeptics and evangelical Christian scholars, especially in the areas of creation versus evolution, the existence of God, and the historical evidence for the resurrection. Through organizations such as Leadership U (http://www.leaderu.com); The John Ankerberg Show; Probe International in Dallas, Texas; the Institute for Creation Research in Santee, California; and others, Christian scholars have vigorously contended against atheists, agnostics, skeptics, evolutionists, cultists, and all varieties of critics of Christianity. Almost invariably, Christian scholars win these debates. Given the nature and importance of the subject matter, these forums leave little doubt that only a person's prejudice or ignorance would cause him to think the Christian position is intellectually lacking.

For example, consider the outcome of a public debate between William Lane Craig and a national spokesman for American Atheists. Dr. Craig has devastated some of the best resurrection critics in the world. He earned a doctorate in philosophy at the University of Birmingham, England, and a doctorate in theology from the Ludwig Maximiliens Universitat-Munchen, Germany, where he was for two years a Fellow of the Alexander von Humboldt-Stiftung, studying the historicity of the resurrection. He is the author of *The Historical Argument for the Resurrection of Jesus* and *Assessing the New Testament Evidence for the Historicity of the Resurrection of Jesus.* Eight thousand people attended this debate in person, and it was broadcast live on over 100 radio stations. Here is the conclusion of the moderator: "In the end it was no contest. Among those who had entered the auditorium that evening as avowed atheists, agnostics, or skeptics, an overwhelming 82 percent walked out concluding that the case for Christianity had been the most compelling. Forty-seven people entered as nonbelievers and exited as Christians...Incidentally, nobody became an atheist."[268]

In another scholarly forum, "Christianity Challenges the University: An International Conference of Theists and Atheists" in Dallas, participants included Christian philosopher Dr. Gary R.

Habermas and Antony G.N. Flew, one of the world's leading philosophical atheists. Dr. Flew has been a visiting professor at 12 universities around the world and has taught at the University of Oxford, the University of Reading in England, and the University of Aberdeen. After this particular series of debates, an invitation was extended to Dr. Flew to debate "The Historicity of the Resurrection: Did Jesus Rise from the Dead?" The invitation was extended to Flew by the philosophy faculty of Liberty University in Lynchburg, Virginia. The debate was held before an audience of 3000 people. Drs. Habermas and Flew were the primary debaters, with participation by W. David Beck, Ph.D., and Terry L. Miethe, Ph.D., dean of the Oxford Study Center, Oxford, England, professor of philosophy at Liberty University, and adjunct professor at Wycliffe Hall, Oxford. Respondents to the debate included three of the world's leading theologians: Wolfhart Pannenberg, who some consider the world's most prominent living systematic theologian, Charles Hartshorne, Ph.D., the noted process theologian, and James I. Packer, Ph.D., a leading evangelical theologian.

Organizers of the debate put together two independent panels of experts in their respective areas of specialty to render a verdict on the debate. The first panel comprised five philosophers who were instructed to judge the debate content and to render a verdict concerning the winner. The second panel comprised five professional debate judges who were told to evaluate the argumentation techniques of the debaters. All ten judges serve on the faculties of American universities and colleges such as the University of Virginia, James Madison University, and the University of Pittsburgh.

What were the results of this two-day debate on the historicity of the resurrection? The decision of the judges was as follows: The panel of five philosophers who judged content cast four votes for Habermas, none for Flew, and one draw. One of these philosophers commented,

I was surprised (shocked might be a more accurate word) to see how weak Flew's own approach was. I expected, if not a new and powerful argument, at least a distinctly new twist to some old arguments...Since the case against the resurrection was no stronger than that presented by Antony Flew, I would think it was time I began to take the resurrection seriously. My conclusion is that Flew lost the debate and the case for the resurrection won.[269]

The panel of professional debate judges voted in favor of Habermas three to two concerning argumentation technique. One of the judges noted,

I am of the position that the affirmative speaker [Habermas] has a very significant burden of proof in order to establish his claims. The various historical sources convinced me to adopt the arguments of the affirmative speaker. Dr. Flew, on the other hand, failed, particularly in the rebuttal. In the head-to-head session, to introduce significant supporters of his position, Dr. Habermas placed a heavy burden on Dr. Flew to refute very specific issues. As the rebuttals progressed, I felt that Dr. Flew tried to skirt the charges given him.[270]

Another professional debate judge observed,

I conclude that the historical evidence, though flawed, is strong enough to lead reasonable minds to conclude that Christ did indeed rise from the dead. Habermas has already won the debate...Habermas does end up providing "highly probable evidence" for the historicity of the resurrection "with no plausible naturalistic evidence against it." Habermas, therefore, in my opinion, wins the debate.[271]

The overall decision of both panels, judging both content and argumentation technique, was a seven to two decision, with one draw, "in favor of the historicity of the resurrection as argued by Habermas."[272] Even some later reviews by skeptics in secular publications agreed that Habermas won the debate, or at least that Flew's critique against the resurrection was inadequate.[273]

The conclusions of the scholarly respondents to the debate were also noteworthy. Wolfhart Pannenberg concluded, "The historical solidity of the Christian witness [to the resurrection] poses a considerable challenge to the conception of reality that is taken for granted by modern secular history. There are good and even superior reasons to claiming that the resurrection of Jesus was a historical event, and consequently the risen Lord himself is a living reality."[274] American philosopher Dr. Charles Hartshorne concluded, "I can neither explain away the evidences to which Habermas appeals, nor can I simply agree with Flew's or Hume's positions," noting "my metaphysical bias is against resurrections."[275]

Dr. James I. Packer declared: "The case for the historical reality of Jesus' bodily resurrection could be made even stronger than Professor Habermas makes it—which, in all conscience, must surely be strong enough already for most people!—by dwelling with more emphasis on the sheer impossibility of accounting for the triumphant emergence of Christianity in Jerusalem..."[276]

---

### 35

## IS CHRISTIANITY NARROW-MINDED AND INTOLERANT FOR TEACHING THERE IS ONE WAY TO GOD, OR IS IT MORE TOLERANT THAN OTHER RELIGIONS?

*It is morally as bad not to care whether a thing is true or not, so long as it makes you feel good, as it is not to care how you got your money so long as you have got it.*
**Edwin Way Teale**

*Truth, like surgery, may hurt, but it cures.*
**Han Suyin**

*It is one thing to wish to have truth on our side, and another to wish sincerely to be on the side of truth.*
**Richard Whately**

We have now addressed some of the evidence that demonstrates Christianity is true. Hundreds of books exist on the subject;

readers should not assume we have covered all bases, but we have, we hope, covered enough to draw our conclusion. Nevertheless, one remaining issue involves the false claim that Christianity is an intolerant religion because it teaches there is only one way to God.

Mortimer Adler pointed out something very important in chapter one of his *Truth in Religion*: "In the sphere of all matters subject to thought and decision, pluralism is desirable and tolerable only in those areas that are matters of taste, rather than matters of truth."[277] Pluralism in truth is not possible when statements of fact or worldviews deny one another. And few would argue that it is wise or profitable to be open-minded about false or harmful alternatives. But most importantly, "such intolerance is entirely a private matter" and requires neither the suppression of false opinions others may hold, nor social or political action requiring others to accept the truth. In other words, truth and public tolerance are fully compatible.[278]

Christianity does teach that faith in Jesus is the only way of salvation, but we will see that it is no less tolerant than other religions. Before we begin, it is important to lay to rest some common misunderstandings pointed out by Dr. Geisler and others. First, Christianity teaches that God loves all people—all unbelievers and all sinners—indeed, far more than they can ever fathom (John 3:16; Romans 5:1-10; Ephesians 3:18; 1 John 4:10). Second, Christianity teaches that God wishes for all men and women to find salvation; He does not desire that any should perish (John 1:12; 1 Timothy 2:4). Third, Christianity teaches that God, because of His great love for people, has graciously provided salvation for everyone—freely, not by works or merit—at no cost, although at tremendous cost to Himself (Ephesians 2:8-9; 1 John 2:2; 3:1; 4:16). Fourth, Christianity teaches that all nations and peoples will eventually be evangelized (Matthew 28:18-20; Revelation 7:9). Fifth, Christianity teaches that although salvation is impossible without Christ, it does not follow that all who do not hear of Christ through missionary activity are necessarily lost. Millions were undoubtedly saved before Christ was born (see Jonah 4:11). And we are promised that anyone who truly wants to know God and earnestly seeks Him will find him (Matthew 7:7-8; Acts 10:34-35; Hebrews 11:6). Thus, if the gospel is not available by missionary work, God can still make it available to those who seek Him—whether by dream, vision, angelic encounter, etc.—as has happened in remote places historically and even in modern societies. Nevertheless, if people are prideful and refuse the light they do have or actively suppress the truth (Romans 1:18-32), then God is not responsible to give them further light, any more than a father is responsible to leave his wealth to an ungrateful and unrepentant son who refuses it (John 3:18-21).[279]

Some skeptics have asked, "If God is a God of love, would He not have revealed Himself to all mankind?" The truth is that God has revealed Himself to all mankind. God has made Himself known to all people in one fashion or another. For example, we find no other religion prefigured and told of in virtually all *other* religions. Numerous books provide many startling examples showing that the concept of one true, supreme God has existed throughout history and exists today in hundreds of cultures around the world. What is involved is often more than just support for monotheism; the basics of *Christianity* are often prefigured and "told" in other religions.[280] It is as if God has placed in every culture certain analogies that point to Jesus, even to His redemption on the cross. God, it seems, has prepared the cultures of the world for the Gospel of Jesus Christ by implanting a basis for the gospel—perhaps something hinted at in Acts 17:26-27. Many incredible cases exist of peoples untouched by the Christian faith who in various ways still knew about the God of heaven as told in the Bible. They already had hints of the Gospel embedded in their religion and culture. As David B. Marshall points out,

> The idea is that the most self-consistently sensible and noble aspects of competitive philosophies and religions (whether instituted before or after Jesus' ministry) not only are fulfilled by Jesus but often cry out (or even implicitly predict) that God would act as traditional Christians

say He has in Jesus…I remember the first time I visited the Temple of Heaven in Beijing, China, 16 years ago. Who was this "Heaven" whom the Chinese worshiped? Why did the emperor come once a year, just like the high priest in Israel, to sacrifice for the sins of the people? As I stood in the most sacred spot in China, it seemed as if a Voice spoke to my heart. "Do you think I just came to China with the missionaries? No. I have been here all along. I made China." Many years of research in China confirmed this to me. Among the tribal cultures of southern China and Taiwan, the Polynesians, and China itself, I came across many examples that confirmed Richardson's [*Eternity in Their Hearts*] thesis. Later, I wrote a book called *True Son of Heaven: How Jesus Fulfills the Chinese Culture*, and spoke around the Pacific Rim on the subject. People in the audience often pointed out further examples of this thesis.

Marshall shows "how persistent and coherent the idea of God is in the pagan cultures of the world," with examples of "redemptive analogies that center on the person of Jesus and on his work on the cross. Many of these come from the more civilized cultures of Asia, and also Marxist, psychologist, feminist, and tribal subcultures of Western civilization."[281]

None of this sounds intolerant or narrow-minded; actually, it sounds about right. However, what bothers some people is the idea there is only one way to God instead of any number of ways. But upon what kind of strange conjecture should it be insisted there be *any number* of ways? What finite creature has the proof needed to demand life function in such a manner? Often, the people who make this complaint aren't even religious; they just don't like the ostensible arrogance. But it's not arrogance because certain concepts (such as truth) can't be arrogant—only people can. If it is true that there is only one way to God, then it's simply true—nothing more, nothing less. Just possibly, we might be arrogant by denying the truth.

Those who think Christianity is intolerant should also find out whether other religions and philosophies are really as tolerant as they claim. In fact, they aren't. *Every* religion claims it is true. This means any belief not in accord with such "truth" must be false. And this means that every religion must condemn every other religion as being wrong whether they admit it publicly or not. One only needs to read their literature to see this.

Every religion also claims it has the only or best way of salvation. Hinduism and Buddhism may teach that everyone will eventually reach the gloomy if somehow desired goal of personal annihilation, but beyond any doubt, they have the best and quickest route there—so much so that any other path is tantamount to a dreadful mistake. (But assuming the truth of their views, one wonders, who wants to die forever anyway?) I (Weldon) have talked to people threatened with reincarnation as an amoeba or worse should they leave a particular religion. All Eastern religions emphasize and defend their unique spiritual importance. Islam also teaches it alone is the true religion. "The true religion with God is Islam" (Sura 3:18), and "Whoso desires another religion than Islam; it shall not be accepted of him; in the next world, he shall be among the losers [shall go to hell]" (3:86). And speaking of tolerance of others, the Bible teaches "love your enemies" (Matthew 5:44) but the Koran teaches that for the unrepentant, "Make war on them until idolatry shall cease and Allah's religion shall reign supreme" (8:39). And, "take neither the Jews nor the Christians for your friends" (5:51). Indeed, the Koran teaches that Islam is to "overcome all religions" (61:9)—so much so that Islam has persecuted Christians, Jews, and polytheists mercilessly, as documented in our *Fast Facts on Islam* (Eugene, OR: Harvest House Publishers, 2001, sections IV and V). Now *that's* intolerance!

And on it goes. We don't know of a single "tolerant" religion. Even religions which actively proclaim their tolerance, like the Baha'i World Faith, only mask their intolerance of other religions by claiming to accept other religions while callously reinterpreting all other religions' "true" teachings as their own unique teachings.

This kind of "tolerance" often conceals the most strenuous intolerance.

So why is Christianity singled out for criticism? If Christianity is the most honest about its beliefs, why should it be maligned while other religions are actually commended for a false tolerance? In fact, one can argue that Christianity is in some ways more tolerant than other religions. To be tolerant is to permit something without protest or interference. Christianity has, with few exceptions, tolerated other religions marvelously well because God commands believers to respect the image of God in all men and to treat all people honorably and with love. The idea of a forced conversion is reprehensible. (Note: not all churches or organizations claiming to be Christian are such.) But other religions have not been so tolerant of Christianity—which has been horribly persecuted by Islam, and to less extent by certain other religions, far more than the reverse. Other religions may attempt to force conversion upon one by various threats including taxation, marginalization, or death. If the history of Christian missions and martyrdom reveal anything, it is that Christianity does not persecute other religions; it is persecuted by other religions.

Followers of other religions are actually more narrow-minded than Christians because they declare they have the truth when they really don't. Christians want people to accept objective truth as confirmed by historical and scientific evidence; others want people to accept errors falsely claimed as truth. The claim that Christianity is true and all non-Christian systems are false is no more narrow than to claim that Hinduism is true and all non-Hindu systems are false. No truth claim is all-inclusive. And,

> The claim to unique truth is shared by every religious
> system that makes truth claims. This is true even of
> "broad," "eclectic" religions. Hindus claim that it is true
> that "there are many ways to God." This appears open-
> minded, but it is just as narrow as the Christian claim. It
> excludes all opposing views...Indeed, all religions claim to
> have *the truth*—even if that truth is that they believe other

noncontradictory religious systems are true also. But if two or more religions embrace the same truth, then they are really one. And that one basic religious system behind them claims to be the true religion to the exclusion of all opposed religious systems. So Christianity's claim to be the true religion is no more narrow than the claim of any other religion.[282]

In essence, when Christianity claims to be fully true and unique, it is not acting differently from any other religion. We can't think of any religion anywhere that tells potential converts that its teachings contain a quantity of errors and have pretty much the same teachings as those in all other religions.

Dr. Geisler is the author of several books that critically evaluate the truth claims of different world views, including *Worlds Apart: A Handbook on World Views*. He correctly points out that every major system of thought has principal truth claims "contrary to those of all other systems" and that therefore, "only one world view can be true." He also points out that a system of thought which is true "must be comprehensive of thought and life," have coherency and consistency in its overall claims, and must correspond to reality—past, present, future, natural, and supernatural. But only Christianity does this. As Dr. Geisler shows in his 800,000 word encyclopedia on Christian evidences, "The only system of truth is the Christian system."[283]

Nevertheless, although the evidence declares the Bible is without error, Christianity itself is not without error. Because Christians are finite and fallible, their understanding of Christianity as a system of truth will have some error in it. In other words, as the evidence shows, Christianity is a system of truth with some error. By contrast, other religions are systems of error with some truth, as the evidence also shows.[284] Here is a vast difference however because unfortunately, the areas in which other religions err are those subjects which are most crucial such as the nature of God, salvation, and man. Thus, Christianity is also unique in its degree of truth when compared to other religions.

The argument that all religions have an equal claim to the truth is ultimately illogical. If all religions have an equal claim to the truth, then no religion has an absolute claim to the truth. In other words, pluralists deny that absolute truth exists in religion. This means they have a relativistic view of truth. But if so, they cut themselves off at the feet. They maintain that relativism is always true, for everyone, everywhere—an absolute truth. In other words, by maintaining that relativism is always true, they appeal to an absolute truth, which denies validity to their relativism and therefore defeats their own position.[285]

Whether or not people like it, there really is only one true religion, only one true way to God. It actually makes sense that if there is only one true God, there would be only one true religion. Christ is the only way to God because as God incarnate, Christ was an absolute authority, and He taught that no one comes to the Father except through Him (John 14:6). Jesus Christ stands alone when compared to the founders of other great religions; if anyone should be heeded in this matter, it should be one with the authority to speak, one who proved His perfect right to make such a claim. And if sin is our problem before God, and Christ alone died for sin, then only He can forgive it. How can Buddha or Muhammad logically forgive anyone's sins when they admitted they were sinners and never claimed the interest or ability?

And there are other considerations. First if there is only one true God, there should only be one true way of salvation because the way of salvation must be consistent with the nature of the one true God—His love, grace, justice, mercy, and truth.

Second, like everything else in the world, salvation must be done correctly to be successful. Our lives are literally filled with examples of the problems we cause when we do things incorrectly. Why should we conclude that doing salvation is any different?

Again, people can be broad-minded or narrow-minded, but not ideas. Ideas are ultimately neither broad nor narrow—they are true or false.

Ironically, it is frequently those people who claim to be accepting and tolerant of almost anything who are most intolerant of one thing—Christian faith. Literally thousands of examples could be cited of bigotry, hypocrisy, narrow-mindedness, and intolerance expressed towards Christians for doing no more than living out the logical consequences of their own religious faith[286] —something that those who malign Christian faith often claim to defend in all religions. Indeed, we challenge our readers to find a single religion anywhere that accepts Christianity as being fully true. Obviously, there are none, because all religions claim they alone are fully true.

Christianity, like other religions, is exclusive, but it is not intolerant. While it seeks to convert others to faith in Christ, it respects the right of all men to choose their own destinies. But if men's destinies are at stake in the issue of salvation, people everywhere should also rejoice that Christians are sharing the good news of the gospel of Jesus Christ. If Christianity really is true, Christians have no other choice.

---

## 36

## WHY IS THE RESURRECTION SO IMPORTANT TO EACH OF US PERSONALLY?

In *The Son Rises*, an excellent text on the historical and logical evidence for the resurrection, Dr. William Lane Craig gives the following anecdote:

> "There ain't gonna be no Easter this year," a student friend remarked to me.
>
> "Why not?" I asked incredulously.
>
> "They found the body," he replied.

Without the resurrection, Christianity is fraudulent and empty, as the Apostle Paul himself emphasized (1 Corinthians 15:14-19). If Jesus remained dead, anything He started died with

Him. The resurrection of Jesus confirms His claims and demonstrates that He holds the key to eternal life. The value of the resurrection for Christians is that it supplies *proof* of our forgiveness by God and full assurance that we will go to an eternal heaven when we die. (Please see John 3:16; 5:24; 8:28-39; Romans 4:25; Colossians 2:13; 1 John 5:13.) No assurance of salvation exists in any religion other than biblical Christianity.

Everyone must die. The Bible teaches that everyone must also live forever—the only question is, Where will they live? The miraculous nature of the Bible, which proves its divine inspiration, Christ's own resurrection, and His infallible pronouncements as God incarnate concerning the true way of salvation are more than sufficient reasons to accept the Christian view that all men and women will spend eternity in either a place called heaven or a place called hell (Matthew 25:46). We all fall short morally, we all sin, we all know we are sinners, we all die. But throughout history, who ever dealt with the problem of sin before God? Not one of the founders of another religion ever claimed and offered proof that he solved the problems of human sin, evil, and death—the most fundamental human problems of all. Only Jesus solved the sin problem and conquered death, so logically, only Jesus is the way of salvation and the way to God and eternal life. J.I. Packer once noted, "No philosophy that will not teach us how to master death is worth two pence to us."

Consider what the Word of God and Jesus Christ, the incarnate Son of God, taught about salvation.

> I am the LORD your God...you shall have no other gods before me (Exodus 20:2-3).

> Before me no god was formed, nor will there be one after me. I, even I, am the Lord, and apart from me, there is no savior (Isaiah 43:10-11).

> I am the way and the truth and the life. No one comes to the Father except through me (John 14:6).

Now this is eternal life: that they may know you, the only true God, and Jesus Christ, whom you have sent (John 17:3).

Salvation is found in no one else, for there is no other name under heaven given to men by which we must be saved (Acts 4:12).

God our savior...wants all men to be saved and to come to a knowledge of the truth. For there is one God and one mediator also between God and men, the man Christ Jesus, who gave Himself as a ransom for all men...(1 Timothy 2:4-6).

If you desire to live forever in heaven with Jesus Christ, the only true Savior, we would encourage you sincerely to pray the following prayer and to seek God with all your heart:

Lord Jesus Christ, I humbly acknowledge that I have sinned in my thinking, speaking and acting, that I am guilty of deliberate wrongdoing, that my sins have separated me from Your holy presence, and that I am helpless to commend myself to You.

I firmly believe that You died on the cross for my sins, bearing them in Your own body and suffering in my place the condemnation they deserved.

I have thoughtfully counted the cost of following You. I sincerely repent, turning away from my past sins. I am willing to surrender to You as my Lord and Master. Help me not to be ashamed of You.

So now I come to You. I believe that for a long time You have been patiently standing outside the door of my heart, knocking. I now open the door. Come in, Lord Jesus, and be my Savior and my Lord forever. Amen.[287]

He is there, He hears, and He answers. If you have prayed this prayer, we encourage you to write us directly at The John Ankerberg Show. We want to help you grow as a Christian. Next, we suggest that you read a modern, easy-to-read translation of the Bible such as the New International Version. Start with the New Testament, Psalms, and Proverbs, and then proceed to the rest of the Scriptures. Also, find a quality church where people honor the Bible as God's Word and Jesus Christ as their personal Lord and Savior. Tell someone of your decision to follow Christ, and begin to grow in your new relationship with God by talking to Him daily in prayer.

> *Seek the LORD while he may be found; call on Him while he is near.*
>
> **Isaiah 55:6**

# NOTES

Unless otherwise indicated, occasional unreferenced citations were taken from various books of contemporary or historical quotations including

Rhoda Tripp, comp., *The International Thesaurus of Quotations* (New York: HarperCollins Publishers, 1996).
Ralph L. Woods, comp. and ed., *The World Treasury of Religious Quotations.*
William Neil, ed., *Concise Dictionary of Religious Quotations* (Grand Rapids, MI: William B. Eerdmans Publishing Company, 1974).
Jonathan Green, comp., *Morrow's International Dictionary of Contemporary Quotations.*

1. Robert Kastenbaum, *Is There Life After Death?* (New York: Prentice Hall, 1984), p. 9 citing Bertrand Russell, *The Autobiography of Bertrand Russell*, vol. 2 (Boston: Little Brown & Co., 1968), pp. 95-96.

2. Isaac Newton, *Mathematical Principles of Natural Philosophy*, trans. Andrew Motte (1714), rev. and ed. Florian Cajori (Berkeley, CA: University of California, 1934), p. 32.

3. Henry Margenau and Roy Abraham Varghese, eds., *Cosmos, Bios, Theos: Scientists Reflect on Science, God and the Origin of the Universe, Life and Homo Sapiens* (LaSalle, IL: Open Court, 1992), p. 139.

4. Cf. Roy Abraham Varghese, *The Intellectuals Speak Out About God* (Dallas: Lewis & Stanley, 1984); Kelly James Clark, ed., *Philosophers Who Believe: The Spiritual Journeys of Eleven Leading Thinkers* (Downer's Grove, IL: InterVarsity, 1993); see http://www.origins.org and note 20 below.

5. For a refutation of the skeptic's critique of the traditional arguments, see Norman L. Geisler, *Baker Encyclopedia of Christian Apologetics* (Grand Rapids, MI: Baker Books, 1998), pp. 275-96; and http://www.origins.org.

6. Blaise Pascal, *Pensées*, trans. W.F. Trotter (http://eserver.org/philosophy/pascal-pensees.txt), p. 222; see www.origins.org/truth/1truth12.html.

7. See www.origins.org.

8. www.leaderu.com/truth/1truth12.html.

9. The one volume abbreviation is Wilhelm Schmidt, *The Origin and Growth of Religion*, trans. H.J. Rose (New York: Cooper Square Publisher, Inc. 1972).

10. Winfried Corduan, *Neighboring Faiths* (Downer's Grove, IL: InterVarsity, 1998), pp. 32-33.

11. See Henry Morris, *Men of Science, Men of Faith* (Santee, CA: Creation-Life, 1990). See also note 6.

12. See Ravi Zacharias, *Can Man Live Without God?* (Nashville, TN: W. Publishing Group, 1994). See also Paul Johnson, "The Necessity of Christianity," http://www.leaderu.com/truth/1truth08.html.

13. Aleksandr Solzhenitsyn, *Warning to the West* (New York: Farrar, Straus & Giroux, LLC, 1986). Some 50 million from Naziism in WWII, including war deaths; at least 60 million from Marxism in Russia, China

and elsewhere; some 50 million from other wars and civil conflicts from 1945–2000, plus some 50 million abortions in America and 100–400 million globally.

14. Paul Johnson, "The Necessity of Christianity," http://www.leaderu.com/truth/1truth08.html.

15. *Los Angeles Times*, June 28, 1986. We could not confirm or disconfirm this research. Some convinced philosophical atheists could pass lie detector tests since the tests aren't perfect and what they measure may reflect conscious belief. But such results, if valid, show that many practical, as opposed to some philosophical, atheists really aren't so sure of their views.

16. Simone de Beauvoir, "A Conversation About Death and God," *Harper's Magazine*, February, 1984, p. 39.

17. Ibid., p. 39.

18. *ABC Evening News*, Nov. 1, 1998.

19. C.G. Jung, *Memories, Dreams, Reflections*, ed. Aniela Jaffe (NY: Vintage, 1965), p. xi.

20. Blaise Pascal, *Pensées* trans. W.P. Trotter (http://eserver.org/philosophy/pascal-pensees.txt), 194. For a critique of atheism and agnosticism, see Phil Fernandes, "Religion and/or Naturalism: New Life for an Old Debate" (www.biblicaldefense.org/Research_Center/articles.htm).

21. C.S. Lewis, *Surprised by Joy* (New York: Harcourt, Brace & World, Inc., 1955), pp. 175, 191.

22. William J. Bennett, *The De-Valuing of America* (Colorado Springs: Focus on the Family Publishing, 1995); Jim Nelson Black, *When Nations Die* (Wheaton, IL: Tyndale House Publishers); S.D. Gaede, *When Tolerance is No Virtue* (Downer's Grove, IL: InterVarsity Press, 1994); Erwin W. Lutzer, *The Necessity of Ethical Absolutes* (Grand Rapids, MI: Zondervan Publishing House, 1981); Dennis McCallum, ed. *The Death of Truth* (Bloomington, MN: Bethany House Publishers, 1996); Paul Vitz, "An American Disaster: Moral Relativism," in William Bentley Ball, ed. *In Search of a National Morality* (Grand Rapids, MI: Baker Books, 1992); Richard M. Weaver, *Ideas Have Consequences* (Chicago: University of Chicago Press, 1984).

23. William D. Watkins, *The New Absolutes* (Minneapolis: Bethany, 1996), pp. 244-46.

24. Lewis Thomas, *The Medusa and the Snail* (New York: Viking Press, 1979), pp. 155-157.

25. From the 1987 Rainbow calendar (Allen, TX: Argus Communications), product #14850.

26. Ibid.

27. Terrance A. Sweeney, *God And* (Minneapolis, MN: Winston Press, 1985), p. 34.

28. Clark, ed., *Philosophers Who Believe*, p. 209.

29. Aldous Huxley, *Ends and Means* (London: Chatto & Windus, 1946), p. 273. Examining the context in which this quotation occurs is instructive. Huxley was frank enough to confess that his desire to be free from the Christian God and morality was based more upon emotional considerations than rational ones: "For myself, as, no doubt, for most of my contemporaries, the philosophy of meaninglessness was essentially an instrument of liberation. The liberation we desired was simultaneously liberation from a certain political and economic system and liberation from a certain system of morality. We objected to the morality because it interfered with our sexual freedom; we objected to the political and economic system because it was unjust. The supporters of these systems claimed that in some way they embodied the meaning (a Christian meaning, they insisted) of the world. There was one admirably simple method of confuting these people and at the same time justifying ourselves in our political and erotic revolt: We could deny that the world had any meaning whatsoever" (p. 270). As Huxley wrote further, "I had motives for not wanting the world to have a meaning; consequently I assumed that it had none, and was able without any difficulty to find satisfying reasons for this assumption. Most ignorance is vincible ignorance. We don't know because we don't want to know. It is our will that decides how and upon which subjects we shall use our intelligence. Those who detect no meaning in the world generally do so because, for one reason or another, it suits their books that the world should be meaningless" (p. 273). But as Ravi Zacharias points out, the atrocities committed historically that are the logical consequences of the antitheistic position are far deeper and more severe than for those (inconsistently) committed in the name of Christianity: "There is nothing in history to match the dire ends to which humanity can be led by following a political and social philosophy that consciously and absolutely excludes God." And, "One of the great blind spots of a philosophy that attempts to disavow God is its unwillingness to look into the face of the monster it has begotten and own up to being its creator." Indeed, "The infrastructure of our society has become mindless and senseless because the foundation upon which we have built cannot support any other kind of structure" (Ravi Zacharias, *Can Man Live Without God?* [Dallas: Word, 1994], XVII, 21-22).

30. Phillip E. Johnson, *Reason in the Balance: The Case Against NATURALISM in Science, Law and Education* (Downer's Grove, IL: InterVarsity, 1995); R.C. Sproul, *Not a Chance: The Myth of Chance in Modern Science* (Grand Rapids, MI: Baker, 1994).

31. D. Russell Humphreys, Ph.D., of Sandia National Laboratories: "It's probably a conservative estimate that there are in the U.S. alone around 10,000 practicing scientists who are biblical creationists." Carl Wieland, "Creation in the Physics Lab," *Creation Magazine*, vol. 15, no. 3, pp. 20-23.

32. http://www.discovery.org/crsc/ and http://www.origins.org.

33. Michael Denton, *Evolution: A Theory in Crisis* (Chevy Chase, MD: Adler & Adler Publishers, Incorporated, 1986), p. 351.

34. Mark Eastman and Chuck Missler, *The Creator Beyond Time and Space* (Costa Mesa, CA: The Word for Today, 1996), p. 27.

35. Hugh Ross, "Astronomical Evidences for a Personal, Transcendent God" in J.P. Moreland, ed., *The Creation Hypothesis: Scientific Evidence for an Intelligent Designer* (Downer's Grove, IL: InterVarsity, 1994), p. 164, citing Paul Davies, *The Cosmic Blueprint: New Discoveries in Nature's Creative Ability to Order the Universe* (New York: Simon & Schuster, 1988), p. 203 and Paul Davies, *Super-Force: The Search for a Grand Unified Theory of Nature* (New York: Simon & Schuster, 1984), p. 243.

36. Stephen C. Meyer, "The Methodological Equivalence of Design and Descent: Can There Be a Scientific 'Theory of Creation'?" in Moreland, ed., *The Creation Hypothesis*, pp. 67-68, citing George Greenstein, *The Symbiotic Universe: Life and Mind in the Cosmos* (New York: William Morrow, 1988), pp. 26-27.

37. Margenau and Varghese (eds.), *Cosmos, Bios, Theos*, p. 83.

38. Francis Crick, *Life Itself: Its Origin and Nature* (New York: Simon & Schuster, 1981), p. 88.

39. Mark Eastman and Chuck Missler, *The Creator Beyond Time and Space* (Costa Mesa, CA: The Word for Today, 1996), pp. 11-12. See especially Alexander Vilenkin, "Did the Universe Have a Beginning?" CALT-68-1772DOE Research and Development Report, California Institute of Technology, Pasadena, November 1992.

40. First quote is cited in Clark Pinnock, *Set Forth Your Case* (Chicago: Moody Press, 1971), p. 9; the second citation is from Jean-Paul Sartre, *Being and Nothingness* (London: Methuen, 1957), p. 566.

41. John Ankerberg and John Weldon, *Fast Facts on Islam* (Eugene, OR: Harvest House Publishers, 2001), pp. 24-25.

42. Frits Staal, "Indian Concepts of the Body," *Somatics: The Magazine/Journal of the Bodily Arts and Sciences*, Autumn/Winter 1983-1984, p. 33.

43. Ajith Fernando, *The Supremacy of Christ* (Wheaton, IL: Crossway, 1995), p. 241.

44. John Ankerberg and John Weldon, *Encyclopedia of New Age Beliefs* (Eugene, OR: Harvest House Publishers, 1996), pp. 220-38.

45. Leslie Paul, *The Annihilation of Man* (New York: Harcourt Brace, 1945), p. 154.

46. Basic Christian doctrines include bibliology, the doctrine of the Bible; theology proper, the doctrine of God (theism, trinitarianism); angelology, the doctrine of angels, elect and reprobate; anthropology, the doctrine of man; harmartiology, the doctrine of sin; ecclesiology, the doctrine of the church; christology, the doctrine of Christ; pneumatology, the doctrine of the Holy Spirit; and eschatology, the doctrine of last things. All these doctrines are unique in key ways when compared with those in other religions. Under the doctrine of salvation, we find the doctrines of depravity, imputation, grace, propitiation/atonement, reconciliation, calling, regeneration, union with Christ, conversion (repentance/faith), justification, adoption, sanctification, eternal security (perseverance), election/predestination, redemption, and death, resurrection, and the final state. Despite the surface similarities of some of these doctrines to those in other faiths, these doctrines are also unique.

47. Richard N. Ostling, "Who Was Jesus?" *Time*, August 15, 1988, p. 37.

48. Norman L. Geisler, *Baker Encyclopedia of Christian Apologetics*, pp.137-38,140.

49. Sura 3:138, "The House of Inram," A.J. Arberry, trans., *The Koran Interpreted* (New York: Macmillan, 1976), 91; Sura, "The Night Journey," in N. J. Dawood, trans., *The Koran* (Baltimore, MD: Penguin, 1972), p. 235.

50. J. M. Rodwell, trans., *The Koran* (New York: Dutton), pp. 244, 384, 423, 460, 468 (Sura 4:106; 40:57; 47:21; 48:2; 110:3).

51. The idea for this considerably revised comparison was suggested by a third party e-mail containing a longer comparison by George Zeller and Steve Van Nattan; most documentation for Muhammad can be

found in our *Fast Facts on Islam*; the remainder in the Koran and Hadith (sayings by Muhammad); Bat Ye'or, *The Dhimmi, Jews and Christians Under Islam* (Madison, NJ: Fairleigh Dickinson University Press, 1985) and *The Decline of Eastern Christianity Under Islam from Jihad to Dhimmitude: 7th–20th Century* (1996); Ibn Warraq, *Why I am Not a Muslim* (Amherst, NY: Prometheus Books Publishers, 1995); and at SecularIslam.org and Answering-Islam.org.

52. Robert O. Ballou, *The Portable World Bible: A Comprehensive Selection from the Eight Great Sacred Scriptures of the World* (New York: The Viking Press, 1968), pp. 134, 147, 151.

53. Houston Smith, *The Religions of Man* (New York: Harper & Row, 1965), p. 99.

54. Clive Erricker, *Buddhism* (Chicago, IL: NTC Publishing, 1995), pp. 2-3.

55. Arthur Waley, trans., *The Analects of Confucius* (New York: Vintage, 1938), p. 130.

56. Yasna, 44:11; Moulton, Ez.368; from Robert E. Hume, *The World's Living Religions* (New York: Charles Scribner's Sons, 1959), p. 203.

57. Tao-The-King, 20:3; 20:5-7 cited in Hume, *The World's Living Religions*, p. 136.

58. In Hume, *The World's Living Religions*, p. 95.

59. Ibid., p. 283.

60. Ibid., pp. 285-86.

61. John Warwick Montgomery, "The Jury Returns: A Juridical Defense of Christianity" in John Warwick Montgomery, ed., *Evidence for Faith: Deciding the God Question* (Dallas: Probe/Word, 1991), p. 319.

62. Frederic R. Howe, "The Role of Apologetics and Evangelism" in Roy B. Zuck, gen. ed., *Vital Apologetic Issues: Examining Reasons and Revelation in Biblical Perspective* (Grand Rapids, MI: Kregel, 1995), p. 26.

63. *Christianity Today*, November 19, 1990, p. 34.

64. Alvin Plantinga, "A Christian Life Partly Lived," in Kelly James-Clark, ed., *Philosophers Who Believe* (Downer's Grove, IL: InterVarsity, 1993), p. 69.

65. *Chattanooga Free Press*, July 23, 1995, p. A-11.

66. L. Neff, "*Christianity Today* Talks to George Gilder," *Christianity Today*, March 6, 1987, p. 35, cited in David A. Noebel, *Understanding the Times: The Religious Worldviews of Our Day and the Search for Truth* (Eugene, OR: Harvest House, 1994), p. 13.

67. Alister E. McGrath, "Response to John Hick" in Dennis L. Okholm and Timothy R. Phillips, eds., *More Than One Way? Four Views on Salvation in a Pluralistic World* (Grand Rapids, MI: Zondervan, 1995), p. 68.

68. Ajith Fernando, *The Supremacy of Christ* (Wheaton, IL: Crossway, 1995), p. 109.

69. Robert A. Morey, *Introduction to Defending the Faith* (Southbridge, MA: Crowne Publications, 1989), p. 38.

70. James Sire, *Why Should Anyone Believe Anything At All?* (Downer's Grove, IL: InterVarsity Press, 1994), p. 10.

71. Norman L. Geisler, "Joannine Apologetics" in Roy B. Zuck, gen. ed., *Vital Apologetic Issues: Examining Reasons and Revelation in Biblical Perspective* (Grand Rapids, MI: Kregel, 1995), p. 37.

72. John Warwick Montgomery, "The Jury Returns: A Juridical Defense of Christianity," in John Warwick Montgomery, ed., *Evidence for Faith: Deciding the God Question*, pp. 319-320.

73. John Ankerberg and John Weldon, *The Facts on Hinduism* (Eugene, OR: Harvest House Publishers, 1991) and *Fast Facts on Islam*, pp. 37-53; John Warwick Montgomery, "How Muslims Do Apologetics" in *Faith Founded on Fact* (New York: Nelson, 1978); David Johnson, *A Reasoned Look at Asian Religions* (Minneapolis, MN: Bethany, 1985); Stuart C. Hackett, *Oriental Philosophy* (Madison, WI: University of Wisconsin Press, 1979); John Ankerberg and John Weldon, "Buddhism" in *Encyclopedia of Cults and New Religions*; John Weldon, *Buddhism* (MA Thesis) on file at Simon Greenleaf University/Trinity International University, Anaheim, CA.

74. John B. Noss, *Man's Religions*, 5th ed., (NY: Macmillan, 1974), p. 417.

75. Chauncey Sanders, *An Introduction to Research in English Literary History* (New York: Macmillan, 1952), pp. 143ff.

76. Josh McDowell, *Evidence That Demands a Verdict* (Nashville, TN: Thomas Nelson Incorporated, rev. 1979), pp. 39-52; and N. Geisler and W. Nix, *A General Introduction to the Bible* (Chicago: Moody Press, 1971), pp. 238, 357-67.

77. Geisler, *Baker Encyclopedia of Christian Apologetics*, p. 529.

78. McDowell, *Evidence That Demands a Verdict*, p. 42; Robert C. Newman, "Miracles and the Historicity of the Easter Week Narratives," in John Montgomery, ed., *Evidence for Faith* (Richardson, TX: Probe Books, 1991), pp. 281-84.

79. F.F. Bruce, *The Books and the Parchments* (Old Tappan, NJ: Revell, 1963), p. 78.

80. F.F. Bruce, *The New Testament Documents: Are They Reliable?* (Downer's Grove, IL: InterVarsity Press, 1971), p. 15.

81. McDowell, *Evidence That Demands a Verdict*, pp. 43-45; Clark Pinnock, *Biblical Revelation: The Foundation of Christian Theology* (Chicago: Moody Press, 1971), pp. 238-39, 365-66; Rene Pache, *The Inspiration and Authority of Scripture*, tr. Helen I. Needham (Chicago: Moody Press, 1969), p. 193, citing Benjamin B. Warfield, *An Introduction to the Textual Criticism of the Old Testament*, p. 12ff.; "The Greek Testament of Westcott and Hort," *The Presbyterian Review*, Vol. 3 (April 1982), p. 356.

82. Montgomery, ed., *Evidence for Faith*, p. 284.

83. John Warwick Montgomery, *Faith Founded on Fact* (New York: Nelson, 1978); F.F. Bruce, *The New Testament Documents: Are They Reliable?*; John Warwick Montgomery, *History and Christianity*; Norman Geisler, *Christian Apologetics*, pp. 322-27.

84. Lee Strobel, *The Case for Christ* (Grand Rapids, MI: Zondervan, 1998), p. 50.

85. Gary R. Habermas, *Ancient Evidence for the Life of Jesus: Historical Records of His Death and Resurrection* (Nashville, TN: Thomas Nelson Publishers, 1984), p. 66.

86. Philip Schaff and Henry Wace, eds., *A Select Library of Nicene and Post-Nicene Fathers of the Christian Church*, 2nd series, vol. 1, Eusebius: Church History, Book 3, Chapter 39, "The Writings of Papias" (Grand Rapids, MI: Eerdmans, 1976), pp. 172-73.

87. Gary R. Habermas, *Ancient Evidence for the Life of Jesus*, pp. 66, 177.

88. Strobel, *The Case for Christ*, p. 120.

89. Gerhard Meier, *The End of the Historical Critical Method* (St. Louis, MO: Concordia, 1977); Josh McDowell, *More Evidence That Demands a Verdict* (San Bernardino, CA: Campus Crusade for Christ, 1972).

90. Gleason L. Archer, Jr., *A Survey of Old Testament Introduction* (Chicago: Moody Press, 1994). Norman L. Geisler and William E. Nix, *A General Introduction to the Bible* (Chicago, Moody Press, 1996); Ellis R. Brotzman, *Old Testament Textual Criticism* (Grand Rapids: Baker, 1994).

91. Geisler, *Baker Encyclopedia of Christian Apologetics*, p. 531.

92. Habermas, *Ancient Evidence for the Life of Jesus*, p. 115.

93. Ibid., pp. 112-13.

94. Gary Habermas, *Ancient Evidence for the Life of Jesus*; cf., F. F. Bruce, *The New Testament Documents: Are They Reliable?* (Downer's Grove, IL: InterVarsity, 1971), chs. 9-10.

95. Interview in Strobel, *The Case for Christ*, p. 65.

96. John Wenham, *Redating Matthew, Mark and Luke*, (Downer's Grove, IL: 1992), pp. 115-19, 136, 183, see pp. xxv, 198, 147, 200, 223, 238-39, 243-45. See also German papyrologist Carsten Peter Thiede, *Eyewitness to Jesus* (New York: Doubleday, 1995).

97. John A. T. Robinson, *Redating the New Testament* (Philadelphia: Westminster, 1976).

98. F. F. Bruce, "Are the New Testament Documents Still Reliable?" *Christianity Today*, October 28, 1978, p. 33.

99. Internet copy.

100. Interview in Strobel, *The Case for Christ*, p. 68.

101. Montgomery, "The Jury Returns: A Juridical Defense of Christianity," in Montgomery, ed., *Evidence for Faith*, pp. 322, 326.

102. J. W. Montgomery, *The Law Above the Law* (Minneapolis, MN: Bethany, 1975), appendix, pp. 91-140.

103. *The Simon Greenleaf Law Review*, Vol. 1 (Orange, CA: The Faculty of the Simon Greenleaf School of Law, 1981-1982), pp. 15-74.

104. Irwin Linton, *A Lawyer Examines the Bible* (Grand Rapids, MI: Baker Books, 1977), p. 45.

105. Lord Chancellor Hailsham, "The Door Wherein I Went," *The Simon Greenleaf Law Review*, Vol. 4, 1984-1985, pp. 28-36.

106. J. Barton Payne, *Encyclopedia of Biblical Prophecy* (Grand Rapids, MI: Baker, 1989), p. 681.

107. Payne, *Encyclopedia of Biblical Prophecy*, p. 7.

108. Norman Geisler, *Christ: The Theme of the Bible* (Chicago: Moody Press, 1969), pp. 31-110.

109. Ibid., p. 88.

110. J. Barton Payne, *Encyclopædia of Biblical Prophecy: The Complete Guide to Scriptural Predictions and Their Fulfillment* (New York: Harper & Row, 1973), p. 27.

111. Ibid., p. 682.

112. Ibid., p. 674.

113. Ibid., p. 682.

114. Ibid., pp. 645-50, 665-70, 682.

115. Ibid., pp. 154-55.

116. John F. Walvoord, *Armageddon: Oil and the Middle East Crisis—What the Bible Says About the Future of the Middle East and of the End of Western Civilization* (Grand Rapids, MI: Zondervan, 1990).

117. Payne, *Encyclopedia of Biblical Prophecy*, p. 369.

118. For a critique see John Ankerberg and John Weldon, *Astrology* (Eugene, OR: Harvest House, 1989) and *The Facts on Psychic Readings* (1997); Nostradamus' inscrutability is perhaps surpassed only by his generosity of meaning.

119. Payne, *Encyclopedia of Biblical Prophecy;* John Urquhart, *Wonders of Prophecy;* Josh McDowell, *Evidence That Demands a Verdict* and *Prophecy—Fact or Fiction?* (Nashville, TN: Thomas Nelson Incorporated, 1981); *Daniel in the Critic's Den* (San Bernardino, CA: Campus Crusade for Christ, 1973); Merrill Unger, *Great Neglected Prophecies;* J.W. Bradbury, ed., *The Sure Word of Prophecy;* Alfred Edersheim, *Prophecy and History* (Grand Rapids, MI: Baker Books, 1980); Willis Beecher, *The Prophets and the Promise;* Sir Robert Anderson, *The Coming Prince* (Grand Rapids, MI: Kregel Publications, 1975), and Arthur Custance's *Hidden Things of God's Revelation* (Grand Rapids, MI: Zondervan, 1979).

120. In our book *The Case for Jesus the Messiah* we discuss these verses in detail.

121. Arthur W. Pink, *The Divine Inspiration of the Bible* (Grand Rapids, MI: Baker Books, 1971), p. 77.

122. Sir Robert Anderson, *The Coming Prince* 10th ed. (Grand Rapids, MI: Kregel, 1977), pp. 81-82.

123. Adapted from Norman Geisler and Ron Brooks, *When Skeptics Ask: A Handbook of Christian Evidences,* (Wheaton, IL: Victor Books, 1990), pp. 114-15.

124. Edersheim; Dr. James Smith, *Prophecy and History: What the Bible Teaches About the Promised Messiah* (Nashville: Thomas Nelson Publishers, 1993); Payne, *Encyclopedia of Biblical Prophecy,* p. 680 (see also, pp. 665-72).

125. Interview in Strobel, *The Case for Christ,* p. 250.

126. Geisler, *Baker Encyclopedia of Christian Apologetics,* p. 93, 95.

127. Ibid, articles on naturalism, miracles.

128. Payne, *Encyclopedia of Biblical Prophecy,* p. 13.

129. Gleason Archer, Jr., *A Survey of Old Testament Introduction* (Chicago, IL: Moody Press, 1974), pp. 326-51.

130. John C. Whitcomb, *Darius the Mede* (Nutley, NJ: Presbyterian and Reformed, 1961); Josh McDowell, *Evidence That Demands a Verdict* (San Bernardino, CA: Campus Crusade for Christ, 1976), p. 308; Peter Stoner, *Science Speaks* (Chicago: Moody Press, 1969), pp. 93-95.

131. Gleason Archer, "Daniel," in Frank E. Gaeblein, ed., *The Expositor's Bible Commentary,* Vol. 7, p. 1298; see also Payne, *Encyclopedia of Biblical Prophecy,* p. 372.

132. Josh McDowell, *Daniel in the Critic's Den: Historical Evidence for the Authenticity of the Book of Daniel,* p. 31.

133. John Ankerberg, et al., *One World: Bible Prophecy and the New World Order* (Chicago, IL: Moody Press, 1991).

134. See ibid. for a brief discussion and note 145.

135. Gleason L. Archer, *Encyclopedia of Bible Difficulties* (Grand Rapids, MI: Zondervan, 1982), pp. 11-12, and personal conversation.

136. Ibid., pp. 24-26.

137. Robert Dick Wilson, *Studies in the Book of Daniel* (Grand Rapids, MI: Baker, 1979).

138. Ibid; Josh McDowell, *Daniel in the Critic's Den: Historical Evidence for the Authenticity of the Book of Daniel,* 1973; K. A. Kitchen, *Notes on Some Problems in the Book of Daniel* (London: Tyndale, 1965), pp. 31-79; Charles Boutflower, *In and Around the Book of Daniel* (Grand Rapids, MI: Kregel, 1977), p. 1370.

139. Arthur Custance, "Some Striking Fulfillment of Prophecy" in *Hidden Things of God's Revelation* (Grand Rapids, MI: Zondervan, 1977), pp. 118-19; see also George T.V. Davis, *Rebuilding Palestine According to Prophecy* and *Fulfilled Prophecies That Prove the Bible*.

140. Ibid., pp. 109-41.

141. Custance, *Hidden Things of God's Revelation*, pp. 121-27; McDowell, *Evidence That Demands a Verdict*, pp. 274-80.

142. Robert W. Manweiler, "The Destruction of Tyre" in Robert C. Newman, ed., *The Evidence of Prophecy: Fulfilled Prediction as a Testimony to the Truth of Christianity* (Hatfield, PA: Interdisciplinary Biblical Research Institute, 1994), pp. 28-30.

143. See the summary in Geisler, *Baker Encyclopedia of Christian Apologetics*, pp. 511-12.

144. An errorless original text applies equally to all Scripture, is limited to proper application of hermeneutics, does not refer to manuscript copies or translations or claim absolute proof or precision (approximations are not errors), etc. See our *Ready With an Answer*, pp. 308-10.

145. Cf. the discussion in Geisler, ed., *Inerrancy* (Grand Rapids, MI: Zondervan, 1980), pp. 45-45, 277-82, as to why "all" is the best translation, not "every." See also H. Wayne House, "Biblical Inspiration in 2 Timothy 3:16" in Roy B. Zuck, gen. ed., *Vital Apologetic Issues* (Grand Rapids: Kregel, 1995).

146. See John Wenham, *Christ and the Bible* (Downer's Grove, IL: InterVarsity, 1973), chapters 1-2, 5, and his chapter in Geisler, ed., *Inerrancy*, pp. 3-38; the classic work is Benjamin B. Warfield, *The Inspiration and Authority of the Bible* (Phillipsburg, NJ: P & R Publishing, 1948); Pierre Ch. Marcel "Our Lord's Use of Scripture" in Henry, ed., *Revelation and the Bible* (Grand Rapids, MI: Baker Book House, 1969), pp. 119-34 and Rene Pache, *The Inspiration and Authority of Scripture* (Chicago: Moody Press, 1966), ch. 18.

147. John Wenham, "Christ's View of Scripture," in Geisler, ed., *Inerrancy*, pp. 14-15.

148. John Murray "The Attestation of Scripture" in N. B. Stonehouse and Paul Woolley, eds., *The Infallible Word. A Symposium* (Grand Rapids, MI: Baker Book House, 1967), pp. 26-27.

149. Montgomery in Montgomery, ed., *God's Inerrant Word* (Bloomington, MN: Bethany, 1974), p. 38.

150. Gleason L. Archer, *Encyclopedia of Bible Difficulties* (Grand Rapids, MI: Zondervan, 1982), pp. 11-12.

151. Robert Dick Wilson, *A Scientific Investigation of the Old Testament*, pp. 13, 20, 130, 162-63; David Otis Fuller, ed., *Which Bible?* (Grand Rapids, MI: Grand Rapids International Publications, 1971), p. 44.

152. J.W. Montgomery, *The Shape of the Past* (Minneapolis, MN: Bethany, 1975), p. 176.

153. "These Scriptures are inerrant (without mistake or error) in all that they affirm and are our final authority in all matters of faith, conduct and history." Benjamin B. Warfield, "A Brief and Untechnical Statement of the Reformed Faith," in *Selected Shorter Writings of Benjamin B. Warfield* (Phillipsburg, NJ: P & R Publishing, 2001).

154. John W. Haley, *Alleged Discrepancies of the Bible* (Grand Rapids, MI: Baker, 1982), p. vii.

155. William Arndt, *Does the Bible Contradict Itself?* (St. Louis: Concordia, 1955), p. xi.

156. Harold O.J. Brown, "The Arian Connection: Presuppositions of Errancy" in Gordon Lewis and Bruce Demarest, eds., *Challenge to Inerrancy* (Chicago: Moody Press, 1984), p. 389.

157. James I. Packer, *Beyond the Battle for the Bible* (Westchester, IL: Cornerstone Books, 1980), p. 43.

158. John Warwick Montgomery, *Myth, Allegory and Gospel* (Bloomington, MN: 1974); C.S. Lewis. "Myth Became Fact" in C.S. Lewis, *God in the Dock* (Grand Rapids, MI: William B. Eerdmans Publishing Company, 1972).

159. Geisler, *Baker Encyclopedia of Christian Apologetics*, p. 692.

160. Ibid.

161. www.reasons.org/resources/apologetics/mysearch.html.

162. Mark Eastman and Chuck Missler, *The Creator Beyond Time and Space* (Costa Mesa, CA: The Word for Today, 1996), pp. 23, 84, 87.

163. Taken from Eastman and Missler, *The Creator Beyond Time and Space*, pp. 87-97. A far more detailed analysis is found in Henry Morris, *The Biblical Basis for Modern Science* (Grand Rapids, MI: Baker, 1984).

164. Ibid., pp. 26-27.

165. The towers collapsed because the force of the entrance (200 tons per plane at 400 miles per hour) literally blew away all fire retardant, causing fire-damaged, unreinforced floors to collapse the walls; 500,000 tons hit the earth's surface in eleven seconds traveling at a speed of 110 miles per hour, collapsing 110

stories into only 9 stories of horrible rubble ("The Twin Towers: Anatomy of a Collapse," The Learning Channel, Feb 6, 2002).

166. Eastman and Missler, *The Creator Beyond Time and Space*, p. 94.

167. Henry M. Morris with Henry M. Morris III, *Many Infallible Proofs* (Santee, CA: Master Books, 1996), pp. 250-51.

168. Eastman and Missler, *The Creator Beyond Time and Space*, p. 156.

169. www.rae.org/index.html.

170. D. James Kennedy, *What If Jesus Had Never Been Born?* (Nashville, TN: Thomas Nelson Publishers, 1994), pp. 1, 8.

171. See our *The Facts on False Views of Jesus* (Eugene, OR: Harvest House Publishers, 1997).

172. See Sir Robert Anderson, *The Coming Prince*, www.yfiles.com, and note 171.

173. Franz J. Delitzsch and Parton J. Gloag, *The Messianic Prophecies of Christ* (Minneapolis: Kloch & Kloch, 1983), pp. 123-24 (See book II, pp. 31-38, for additional important literature).

174. G. K. Chesterton, *The Everlasting Man* (Garden City, New York: Image, 1985), p. 272.

175. Ibid., p. 274.

176. The word used by Matthew was often used of Roman soldiers, not just temple officers. See Lee Strobel, *The Case for Christ*, p. 287.

177. Strobel, *The Case for Christ*, p. 312.

178. Ibid., p. 314.

179. Ibid., p. 318.

180. Ibid., p. 320.

181. Interview in Strobel, *The Case for Christ*, p. 11.

182. William E. Lecky, *History of European Morals from Augustus to Charlemagne*, vol. 2 (New York: D. Appleton and Co., 1903), pp. 8-9 in Josh McDowell, *More Than a Carpenter* (Wheaton, IL: Tyndale/Living Books, 1983), p. 28.

183. John Warwick Montgomery, *History and Christianity* (Downer's Grove, IL: InterVarsity, 1965), p. 63.

184. McDowell, *More Than a Carpenter*, p. 30.

185. James W. Sire, *Why Should Anyone Believe Anything At All?* (Downer's Grove, IL: InterVarsity, 1994), pp. 133-35.

186. Ernest R. Hilgard et al., *Introduction to Psychology* (New York: Harcourt Brace Jovanovich, 1971), p. 472.

187. Strobel, *The Case for Christ*, p. 206.

188. Montgomery, *History and Christianity*, p. 65.

189. Ibid., pp. 65-66.

190. *Encyclopædia Britannica*, s.v. "Jesus Christ."

191. *Carl Henry at His Best* (Grand Rapids, MI: Zondervan Publishing House, 1990), p. 203.

192. Pascal, *Pensées*, 801-802.

193. Philip Schaff, *History of the Christian Church*, vol. 1, Apostolic Christianity (Grand Rapids, MI: Eerdmans, 1978), p. 109.

194. Strobel, *The Case for Christ*, p. 198.

195. C. S. Lewis, *Miracles: A Preliminary Study* (London: Collins/Fontana, 1970), p. 113.

196. C. S. Lewis, *Mere Christianity* (New York: Macmillan, 1971), p. 56.

197. Ajith Fernando, *The Supremacy of Christ*, p. 243.

198. Adapted from Norman L. Geisler, *The Battle for the Resurrection* (Nashville, TN: Thomas Nelson, 1984), p. 141, references added.

199. Norval Geldenhuys, *Commentary on the Gospel of Luke* (Grand Rapids, MI: Eerdmans, 1975), p. 628.

200. Interview in Strobel, *The Case for Christ*, p. 108.

201. William Lane Craig, *The Son Rises: Historical Evidence for the Resurrection of Jesus* (Chicago: Moody Press, 1981), pp. 128-30.

202. Ibid., p. 131.

203. Interview in Strobel, *The Case for Christ*, p. 338.

204. Strobel, *The Case for Christ*, pp. 338-41, 344.

205. In Josh McDowell, *More Than a Carpenter*, p. 86, citing *Chamber's Encyclopædia*, vol. 10 (London: Pergamon Press, 1966), p. 516.

206. www.yfiles.com/sign.htm.

207. A. Harnack, "Alexandria, School of," *The New Schaff-Herzog Encyclopædia of Religious Knowledge*, vol. 1 (Grand Rapids, MI: Baker, 1977), pp. 124-25, 347 and L. Russ Bush, ed., *Classical Readings in Christian Apologetics: A.D. 100–1800* (Grand Rapids, MI: Zondervan, 1983), p. 31.

208. Bush (ed.), *Classical Readings in Christian Apologetics: A.D. 100–1800*, pp. 195-98.

209. American Antiquarian Society, Early American Imprints, No. 8909 (1639–1800 A.D.), p. 3.

210. Frank Morison, *Who Moved the Stone?* (Downer's Grove, IL: InterVarsity Press, 1969), pp. 9-10.

211. Ibid., p. 10.

212. Ibid., p. 11.

213. In Josh McDowell, *Evidence That Demands a Verdict* (San Bernardino, CA: Here's Life Publishers, rev. ed. 1979), p. 351.

214. Ibid., p. 368.

215. C. S. Lewis, *Surprised by Joy*, pp. 175, 191.

216. Ibid., pp. 228-29.

217. McDowell, *Evidence That Demands a Verdict*, p. 373.

218. Personal conversations with Dr. Weldon, March 26-28, 1990.

219. The John Ankerberg Show, transcript of a debate between Dr. John Warwick Montgomery and John K. Naland, televised April 1990, p. 39.

220. John Warwick Montgomery, "Introduction to Apologetics" class notes, Simon Greenleaf School of Law, Anaheim, CA, January 1986.

221. Malcolm Muggeridge, *Jesus: The Man Who Lives* (New York: Harper & Row, 1978), pp. 7, 184, 191.

222. W. Ward Gasque, "An Introduction to the Man and His Work" (http://webminister.com/ramsay/rbio02.shtml).

223. In McDowell, *Evidence That Demands a Verdict* (1972 ed.), p. 366.

224. William M. Ramsay, *St. Paul the Traveler and the Roman Citizen*, p. 8 in Fred Williams, *Evidences of the Bible* (www.evolutionfairytale.com/bibleevidences/archeology.html).

225. W.J. Sparrow-Simpson, *The Resurrection in Modern Thought* (London, 1911), p. 405, from Wilbur M. Smith, *Therefore Stand: Christian Evidences* (Grand Rapids, MI: Baker, 1972), p. 365.

226. Strobel, *The Case for Christ*, p. 15,16,32, 356-59, 361-65.

227. www.yfiles.com/sign.htm.

228. www.risenjesus.com.

229. Joseph Thayer, *Thayer's Greek English Lexicon of the New Testament* (Grand Rapids, MI: Baker, 1982), p. 617; James Hope Moulton and George Milligan, *The Vocabulary of the Greek Testament Illustrated from the Papyri and Other Non-Literary Sources* (Grand Rapids, MI: Eerdmans, 1980), p. 628; Spiros Zodhiates, *The Hebrew-Greek Key Study Bible* (Grand Rapids, MI: Baker, 1985), p. 71; Kurt Aland et al., *The Greek New Testament* (New York: American Bible Society, 1968), p. 179.

230. Strobel, *The Case for Christ*, p. 17.

231. Michael Green, *Man Alive!* (Downer's Grove, IL: InterVarsity), 1969 p. 54.

232. Wilbur M. Smith, *Therefore Stand: Christian Apologetics* (Grand Rapids, MI: Baker, 1972), p. 425, see also p. 584.

233. *Encyclopædia Britannica Micropaedia*, vol. 4, s.v. "Hugo Grotius" and references.

234. Hugo Grotius, *The Truth of the Christian Religion* (1624 rev. edition p. 99).

235. In Josh McDowell, *Evidence That Demands a Verdict*, pp. 201-02.

236. J.N.D. Anderson, *Christianity: The Witness of History* (London: Tyndale Press, 1970), p. 90.

237. Ibid., p. 105.

238. John Stott, *Basic Christianity* (London: InterVarsity Fellowship, 1969), p. 47.

239. Irwin H. Linton, *A Lawyer Examines the Bible: A Defense of the Christian Faith* (San Diego: Creation Life Publishers, 1977), pp. 13, 16, 45, 50, 120, 192, 196.

240. Smith, *Therefore Stand*, p. 423.

241. Linton, *A Lawyer Examines the Bible*, p. 36.

242. Josh McDowell, *More Than a Carpenter,* p. 97.

243. John Warwick Montgomery, *The Law Above the Law* (Minneapolis, MN: Bethany, 1975), pp. 132-33. (Greenleaf's *Testimony of the Evangelists* is reprinted as an appendix.)

244. Linton, *A Lawyer Examines the Bible,* p. xxiv.

245. Ibid., p. 242; Sherlock's text is reproduced herein.

246. Sir Lionell Luckhoo, *What Is Your Verdict?* (Fellowship Press, 1984), p. 12, cited in Ross Clifford, *Leading Lawyers Look at the Resurrection* (Claremont, CA: Albatross, 1991), p. 112.

247. Dale Foreman, *Crucify Him: A Lawyer Looks at the Trial of Jesus* (Grand Rapids, MI: Zondervan, 1990), pp. 176-78, cited in Clifford, *Leading Lawyers Look at the Resurrection,* p. 127.

248. Francis J. Lamb, "Miracle and Science: Bible Miracles Examined by the Methods, Rules and Tests of the Science of Jurisprudence as Administered Today in Courts of Justice," *Bibliotheca Sacra,* 1909, p. 284, cited in Clifford, *Leading Lawyers Look at the Resurrection,* p. 128.

249. Clifford, *Leading Lawyers Look at the Resurrection,* pp. 128-32.

250. Lord Chancellor Hailsham, "The Door Wherein I Went," ("On His Conversion and the Truth of Christian Faith"), The Simon Greenleaf Law Review, vol. 4.

251. Lord Diplock in *The Simon Greenleaf Law Review,* vol. 5, pp. 213-16. See Thomas Sherlock, "The Trial of the Witnesses of the Resurrection of Jesus" (rpt.) in John Warwick Montgomery, *Jurisprudence: A Book of Readings,* 1974.

252. Linton, *A Lawyer Examines the Bible,* p. 186.

253. Ibid., pp. 14-20 and Stephen D. Williams, *The Bible in Court: A Brief for the Plaintiff* (1925); Judge Clarence Bartlett, *As a Lawyer Sees Jesus: A Logical Analysis of the Scriptural and Historical Record* (Cincinnati, OH: New Life/Standard Publishing, 1960), pp. 127-28; William Webster, "The Credibility of the Resurrection of Christ Upon the Testimony of the Apostles" (1735), *The Simon Greenleaf Law Review,* vol. 6 (1986-1987), pp. 99-145.

254. See the Council for Christian Colleges and Universities scholarly and professional societies list at: www.cccu.org/resources/profsoc.htm and the list at http://tycho.bgsu.edu/~dlaird/christprofsoc.html. See also the Victoria Institute of Great Britain, and the Creation Research Society in the U.S.

255. See their essays in Kelly James Clark, ed., *Philosophers Who Believe: The Spiritual Journeys of Eleven Leading Thinkers.*

256. Wilbur M. Smith, *The Supernaturalness of Christ* (Grand Rapids, MI: Baker, 1974, rpt.), p. 220.

257. Interview in Strobel, *The Case for Christ,* p. 44.

258. Strobel, *The Case for Christ,* p. 358.

259. Smith, *The Supernaturalness of Christ,* p. 205.

260. Smith, *Therefore Stand,* p. 398.

261. Gary Habermas, *Ancient Evidence for the Life of Jesus: Historical Records of His Death and Resurrection* (New York: Nelson, 1984), pp. 20-21.

262. J. Orr, *International Standard Bible Encyclopædia,* vol. 3, 1st ed., p. 1664; see also J. Orr, *The Resurrection of Jesus* ( Joplin, Mo: College, 1972 repr.), pp. 9-30.

263. G. Hanson, *The Resurrection and the Life* (New York: Revell, 1911), p. 24.

264. Smith, *Therefore Stand,* p. 451.

265. John Warwick Montgomery, *History & Christianity,* p. 77.

266. J. Lilly, "Alleged Discrepancies in the Gospel Accounts of the Resurrection," *Catholic Biblical Quarterly,* vol. 2, 1940, p. 99.

267. Strobel, *The Case for Christ,* p. 301.

268. Strobel, *The Case for Christ,* p. 277; Strobel was the moderator.

269. Terry L. Miethe, ed., *Did Jesus Rise from the Dead? The Resurrection Debate* (New York: Harper & Row, 1987), xiv.

270. Ibid.

271. Ibid., p. xv.

272. Ibid.

273. Ibid., p. 254.

274. Ibid., pp. 134-35.

275. Ibid., 142.

276. Ibid., 149.

277. From book excerpts at Amazon.com, text, p. 2.

278. Ibid., text, p. 3.

279. Geisler, *Baker Encyclopedia of Christian Apologetics*, p. 784.

280. Don Richardson, *Eternity in Their Hearts* (Cincinnati, OH: Gospel Light Publications, 1981), and *Peace Child;* David B. Marshall, *Jesus and the Religions of Man* and *True Son of Heaven: How Jesus Fulfills the Chinese Culture* (Enumclaw, WA: WinePress Publishing, 1996); C. H. Kang and Ethel Nelson, *The Discovery of Genesis: How the Truths of Genesis Were Found Hidden in the Chinese Language* (Saint Louis, MO: Concordia Publishing House, 1979) and G.K. Chesterton, *The Everlasting Man* (San Francisco: Ignatius Press, 1993) and *Orthodoxy* (Allen, TX: Resources for Christian Living, 1985).

281. Author comments at Amazon.com. See reviews of Don Richardson, *Eternity in Their Hearts.*

282. Geisler, *Baker Encyclopedia of Christian Apologetics*, p.785.

283. Ibid.

284. Ibid.

285. Ibid., p. 601.

286. In science see Jerry Bergman, *The Criterion* (Richfield, MN: Onesimus Publishers, 1984).

287. Taken from John Stott, *Becoming a Christian* (Downer's Grove, IL: InterVarsity, 1950), p. 25-26.